AF380868

Colour Theory *for* Artists

Colour Theory
for Artists

Ian Goldsmith

ilex

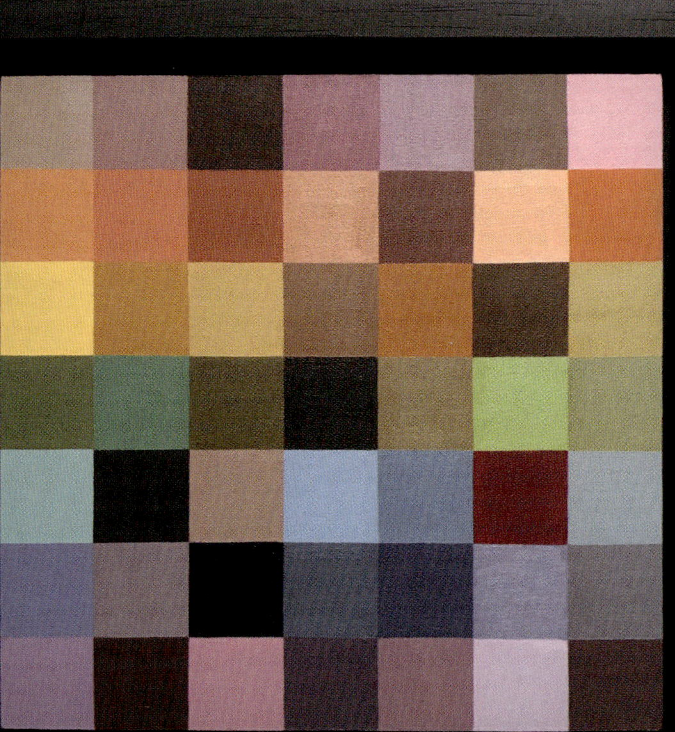

Contents

Introduction

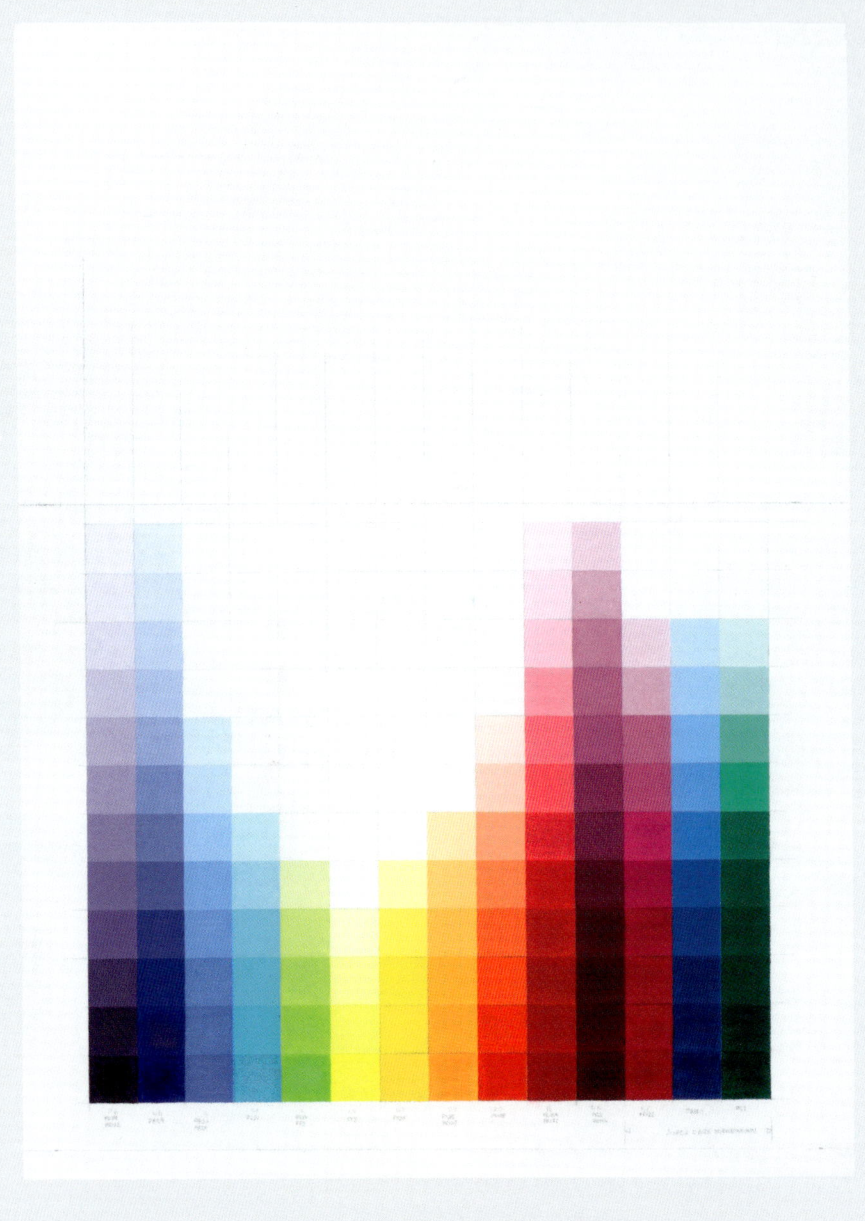

In conducting the research and experimentation needed to write this book, I have invariably found that the more I learn about colour, the more I realise I have yet to learn, as it is such a vast and complex subject.

My very patient physics teacher in secondary school once said, after trying to explain an equation to me for what was most likely the hundredth time, that we don't have to know *why* something is what it is, sometimes we just have to accept that it is what it is. However, I've never been satisfied with that answer, and I've always wanted to peek behind the proverbial curtain of how something works. Perhaps a slight laziness and a desire to look for time-saving techniques has also led me, ironically in this case, to spend a very long time looking for shortcuts in mixing colour, and to find a basic framework that could underpin the process and simplify it.

In my experience, a lot of what is written about colour theory is highly technical and concerned with the physics of colour and light, or how we perceive colour via the biological structures of the eye and brain. This book is written for artists and, as such, I have largely concentrated on how colour theory can be applied in practice, to give you a glimpse of some of the principles that tie together the colours we use, and to help you better understand how colour interacts in paint. I have therefore tried to avoid or to simplify any subjects that are overly scientific and theoretical.

Introduction

If you're anything like me, you might be inclined to skip the introduction to this book and skim through the rest, looking for the good bits and pictures. So, I'm hoping you're not like me, but more like my lovely wife, who carefully reads everything, including the introduction. I've tried to lay this book out in a methodical manner to help the reader build on their knowledge as they progress, so the best way to approach it is from start to finish.

All the diagrams in this book are hand-painted with colours that are freely available to most artists, and I've tried to keep the palette simple and affordable where I can. Most of these are everyday colours that are often available to the student, as well as in more expensive professional ranges of oil colours. While I have in this book concentrated largely on oil colours, readers should note that the principles should remain the same for acrylic paints and watercolours too.

The language around colour is often up for debate, and so the terminology in this book won't always be orthodox (because I'm not sure there is an orthodoxy). But I believe the principles are sound, and any area in which I have challenged a norm is only to make the book as helpful as possible to the artists reading it. I haven't reinvented the wheel exactly, although I have adjusted some colour ones.

Most of what I think I've discovered when mixing colours (in 'Eureka!' moments that often have me excitedly running around the room) have, of course, turned out later to have already been discovered by someone else, but I think there are also some genuine contributions to add to the subject in here too. Most importantly, I am bringing them all together here in one volume, which I hope will at least be of help as a compendium of tips and techniques for artists.

What I've written about has been the result of thousands of hours of trial and error, which has been helped tremendously by friends, colleagues and the generosity of professionals and experts in their specialised subjects, and for their help I am so very grateful.

Any new work like this may draw criticism, but I hope it will be received in the spirit in which it is written: a contribution to the ongoing discussion about colour and how it is understood and taught. With that in mind, I hope you enjoy what you discover here. If it sparks thoughts that help you build upon what you find here and improve upon what I've written, even better.

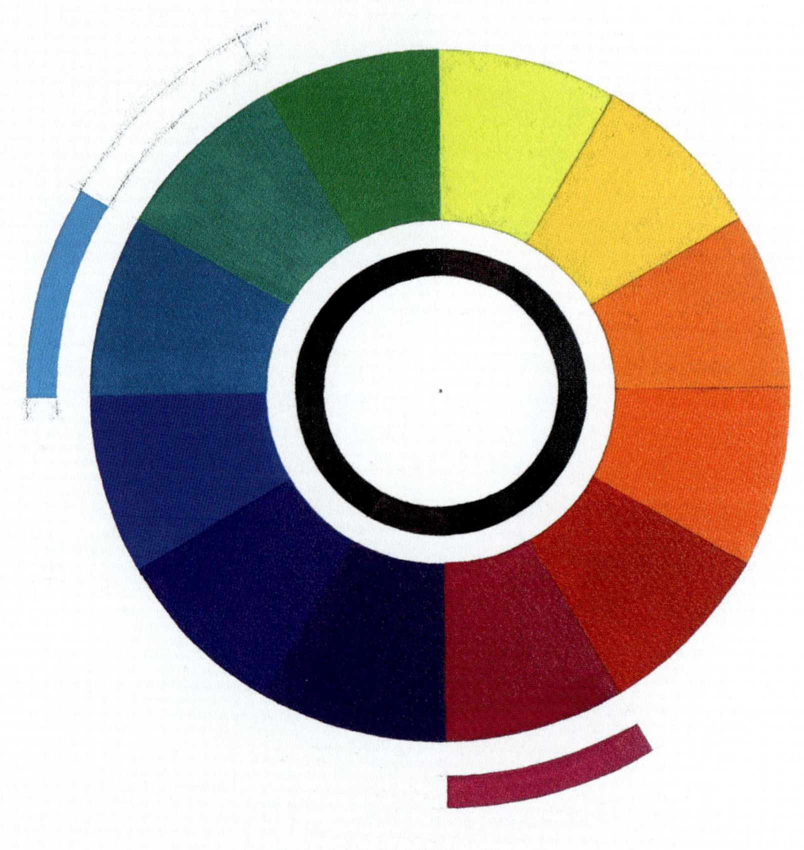

How *to* Use This Book
Creating colour wheels that work for you

A colour wheel, or ring or circle, is simply a tool with which we can hope to better understand colour relationships. By that metric, there can, of course, be many different versions, and a new colour wheel can be created to express whatever aspect of colour you wish to explore. I've made lots of them over my years of creating art, and have refined and improved them along the way, as they've assisted me to understand colour better. There are wheels that help explain the spectrum, rings that explain complementary colour relationships and rings that show colour adjacency or the continuum or hues. I highly advise you to experiment and to use them as a stepping stone to a better understanding of colour.

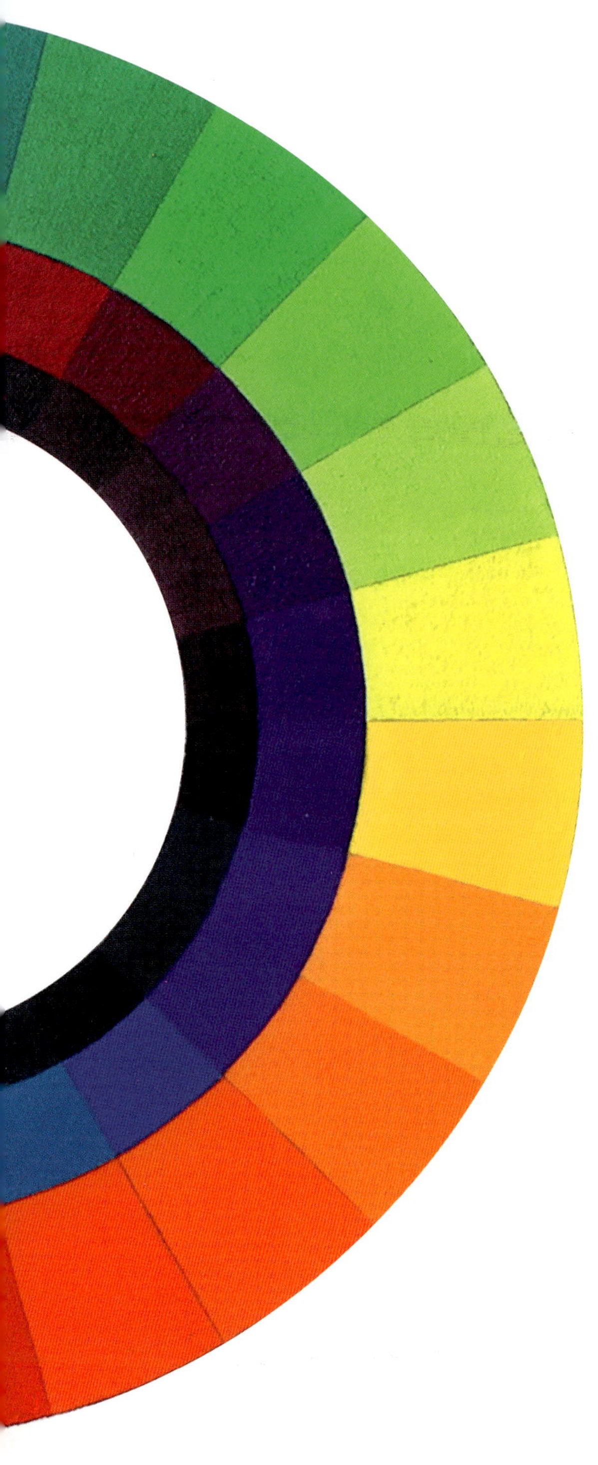

Take the ring on page 12, for example. I started it with the aim of creating a standard 12-section ring with all the primary and secondary colours in temperature pairs, but using colours that when mixed with their opposite colour on the ring would create colour neutrality and so prove they are true complementaries of one another.

As it turned out, the results weren't at all what I wanted, visually at least. It works (as the black ring of mixes in the centre proves), but it looks out of balance. The green is too dark and jars against the cool yellow, and primary and secondaries are so similar in value that it's difficult to tell them apart. However, what it does illustrate rather well is the way in which the warm and cool colours split into two hemispheres. And the difference in values between the cool and warm sides is stark, indicating the importance of blue in creating darker values.

I also learnt that purple really doesn't like being forced into making black. The yellow, being a lighter value (as we don't have a truly transparent primary yellow), unavoidably makes the purple lighter when added, which happily reinforces the results of another experiment I had done previously, but it also questions purple as being a good starting point for mixing black. Warm red and cool blue-green made the best black here – colours much closer in value to one another.

So, I didn't get the results I may have wanted, but the experiment did teach me more about the relationships of colour, and that's exactly why everyone should make a colour ring. I hope you find the charts in this book useful, but if you really want to learn about colour you need to play with it, and the more you play and experiment with it, the more you will learn.

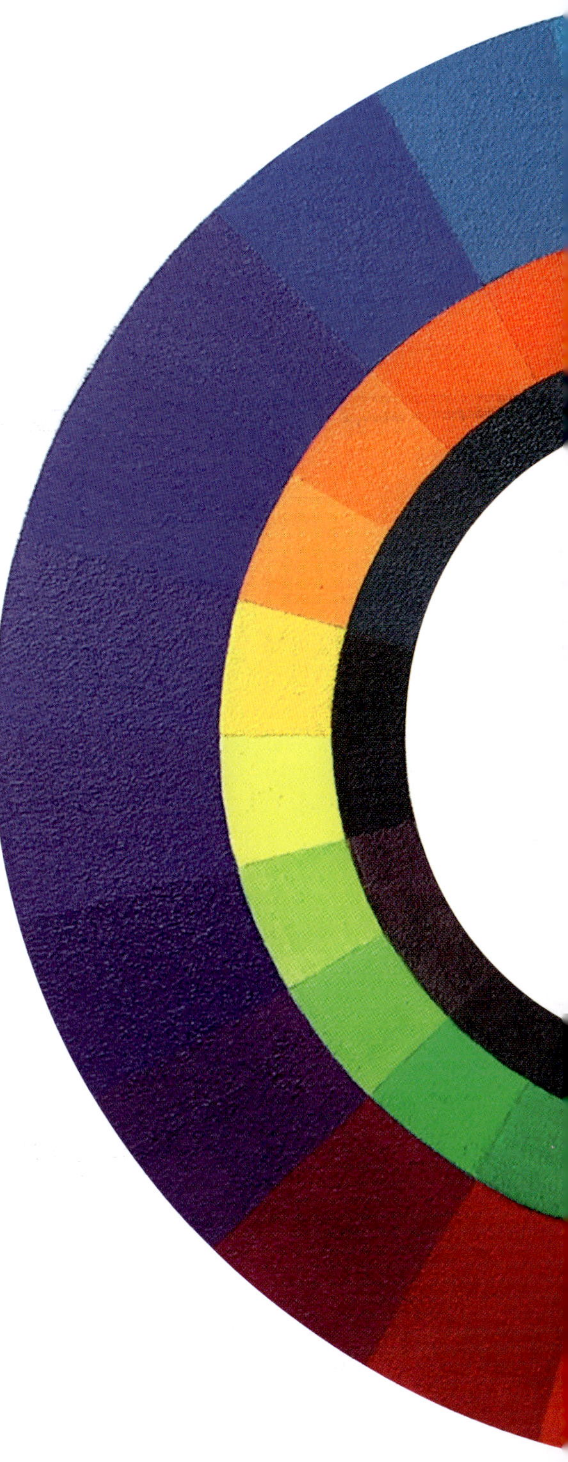

Glossary *of* Colour Terms

The terminology used to describe
colours can be confusing, and this isn't
helped by the fact that not all aspects
of colour have universally accepted
words to describe them. In this book,
I have tried to use a consistent set of
words but have included alternatives
where necessary.

This isn't an exhaustive glossary,
and it won't cover all the strange and
romantic-sounding terms you're likely
to find in the field of art and colour. But
it should help to demystify some of the
terms used later in this book and can
easily be referred back to.

Right A diagram showing the primaries and
their influence over the temperature of the
secondaries they create. For further detail,
see page 100.

Introduction

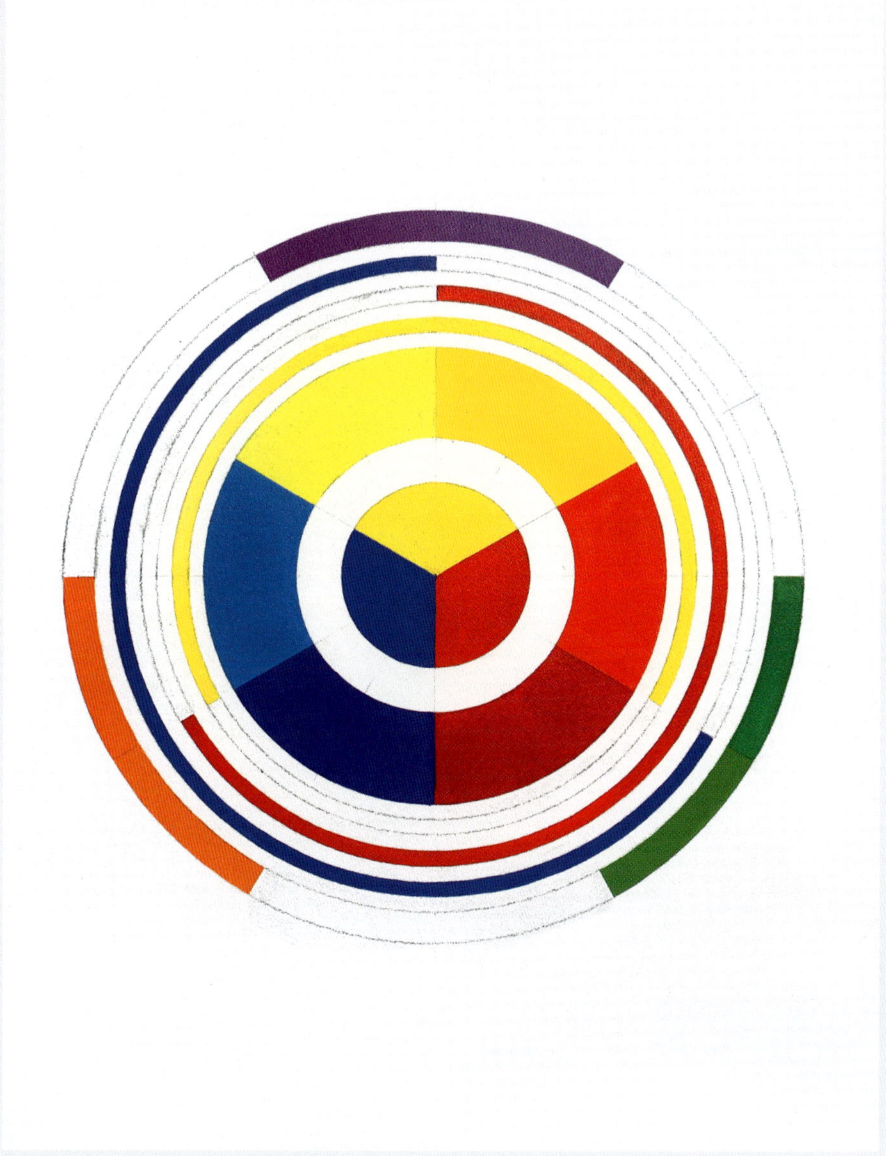

Bias – In this book, bias is a visually identifiable influence from another colour. For example, warm red would be said to have a yellow or orange bias. Related terms are overtone, temperature and adjacency. See page 68.

Chroma – The Greek word for colour. A term made popular by A.H. Munsell to describe the purity or vibrancy of a colour. In this book, I use the more common synonymous term saturation.

Colour – A very broad term, although its most common use is largely synonymous with hue.

Colour adjacency – Describes the relationship between a colour and its neighbour on the spectrum. For instance, yellow would be a colour adjacent to green and red.

Colour Index Name and Number – Codes assigned to all pigments used in paints, printed on paint labels for easy identification of pigment colours. Published by the Society of Dyers and Colourists (SDC) and American Association of Textile Chemists and Colorists (AATCC). See page 159.

Complementary – Often, the colours opposite one another on a colour wheel, when added together, will diminish saturation and lead to colour neutrality, in the form of a grey or black. Not to be confused with complimentary, which means to say something nice.

Gesso – Traditionally, a combination of glue made from the dried skins of rabbits and white powder, such as marble dust or chalk. Today, it more often refers to a preparatory acrylic primer used as a ground (base) on which to apply paint.

Below Greyscale

0% (Black)   100% (White)

                Introduction

Greyscale – Academically, this is often represented as 0% (black) to 100% (white), with a range of greys (the greyscale) in between. In the reprographics industry, this is reversed as 0% (white) to 100% (black). Rather confusingly, in art and design, both can be used. Greyscale can also refer to an image that is drawn, painted or produced entirely in black and white.

Ground – The primary layer of paint or primer (gesso) applied to a surface intended for painting. It is often white but can be any colour.

Hue – A synonym for colour, but more specifically colour from the family of pure spectrum colours: red, orange, yellow, green, blue and purple. See page 31.

Impossible colours – Colours that shouldn't exist, such as a red-green or a yellow-blue. This, like opponent colour theory, is an area of colour perception rather than physical colour mixing in paint, but I love the idea of there being 'impossible colours', so thought I'd mention it here.

Mass tone and undertone – Mass tone is a common term for the colour of undiluted paint, seen when applied thickly. The undertone is how the colour is seen when brushed out thinly or diluted to a wash consistency. Some paints will appear different in colour when applied thickly as opposed to when applied thinly.

Medium – Any substance with which art is created. In paint, it usually refers to the binder used to hold the pigment together, as in oil colour, watercolour, egg tempera or acrylic.

Neutral – In this book, a colour that has no discernible hue/colour, or a colour that has had its 'matched complementary colour' added to it to diminish saturation, usually resulting in an increase in visible darkness as well as diminishing saturation.

Opacity/transparency – The difficulty or ease with which light passes through a substance. Opaque lets no light pass through; transparent lets almost all light pass through. See page 76.

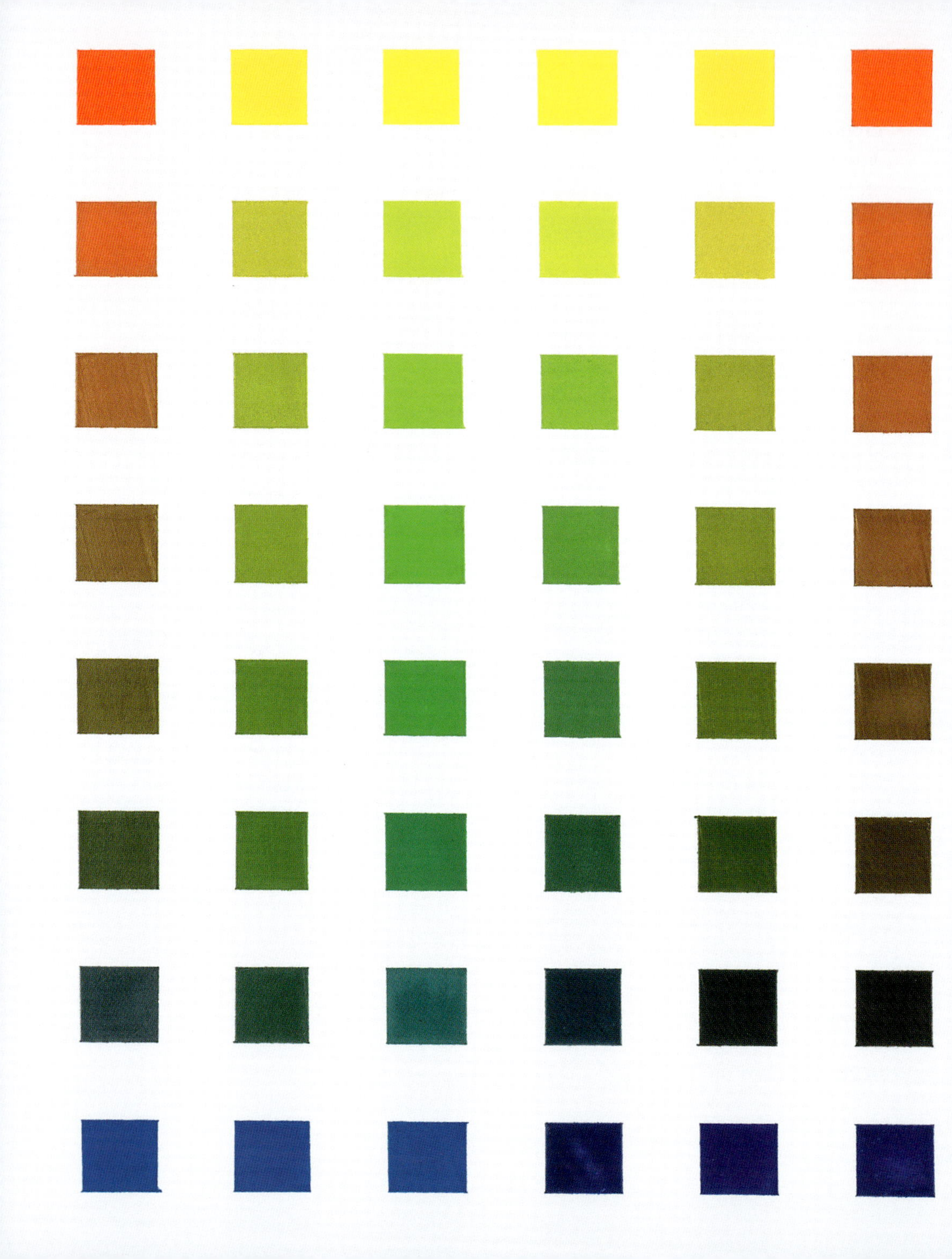

Opponent colour – A colour that is the retinal after-image of another colour. If you stare at a colour long enough and then look away and blink, you should see another colour when you blink; this is its opponent colour (red v green, blue v yellow, black v white). A theory first proposed in 1892 by the wonderfully named Ewald Hering (1834–1918), and one that is closely linked to complementary colour theory, although the former deals with the perception of a colour and the latter with the physical creation of a colour by mixing paint.

Primary – A pure spectrum colour that cannot be mixed by combining other spectrum colours. In paint, these are usually said to be red, blue and yellow. See page 88.

Saturation – Also sometimes referred to as chroma, vibrancy or colour purity. Full saturation would be a colour that is at its most pure and vibrant, neither diminished by excess light nor darkness. See page 52.

Secondary – A colour made up of two primary colours. In paint, there are three secondary colours: orange, green and purple.

Semi-transparent – A substance that allows some light through, but not all, rendering it neither completely transparent nor opaque.

Shade – A colour with black added, with the result being increased darkness and decreased saturation.

Tertiary – In this book, I somewhat unconventionally use this term to mean a colour comprising all three primary colours – that is, a secondary (two primaries in combination) plus the primary not used to create the secondary, or all three different primaries mixed in some ratio. In other works on colour, tertiary can also mean a primary mixed with an adjacent secondary, for example, a red-orange or blue-green. To my mind, this makes little sense, as a different colour is not created – red-orange is still orange – hence my unconventional, but I think more useful, use of tertiary within this context.

Tint – A colour with white added, with the result being increased lightness and decreased saturation.

Tone – A colour with grey added, the result being an adjustment in the value of the colour and decreased saturation. Tone can also mean any combination of black and white used to create a grey – that is, a point between black and white on the tonal range.

Tonal range – The levels of grey between an image's darkest to lightest point. Often means the complete tonal range between white and black, but it can be any section of that range. Tone and value are often synonymous in conversations around light and darkness, but tone more properly refers to greys and to colours in combination with greys.

Value – How relatively dark or light a hue is. See page 36.

Visible spectrum (here often just called 'the spectrum') – The range of component colours of light that we see when light is divided when travelling through a prism and projected onto a surface or seen in a rainbow. It was first demonstrated in experiments by Isaac Newton (1643–1727), as detailed in his seminal work *Opticks*, published in 1704. Thanks to James Clerk Maxwell (1831–79), we also now know that coloured light is in fact a form of visible electromagnetic radiation, and a tiny part of a vast spectrum of electromagnetic radiation which ranges from radio waves to X-rays. Humans can see the bit from around 750 nanometers (red) to around 380 nanometers (violet). It is this range of wavelengths of visible electromagnetic radiation that gives us the spectrum of visible light, and from this we get all the colour we see in the world around us.

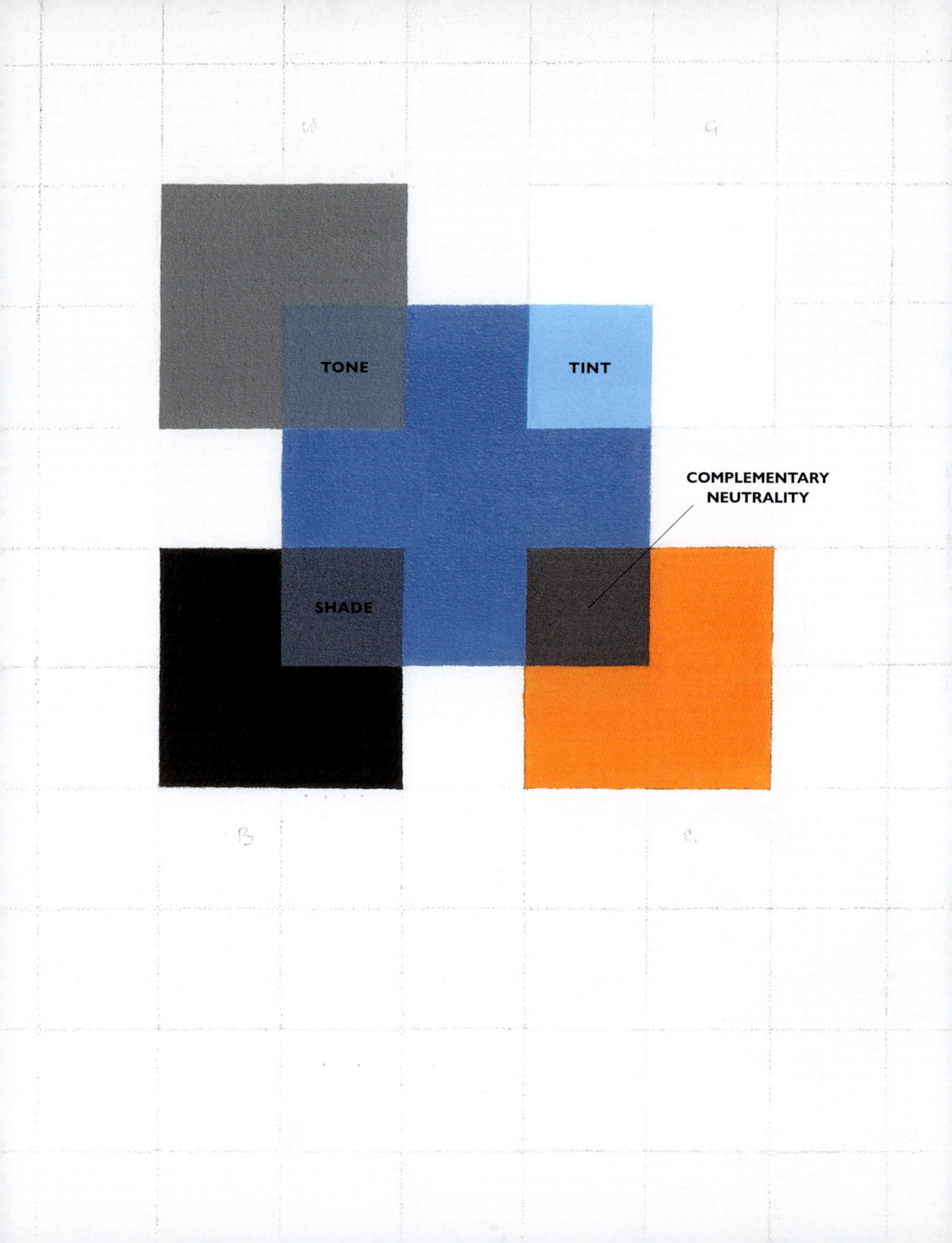

TONE
TINT
SHADE
COMPLEMENTARY
NEUTRALITY

1

The Attributes
of Colour

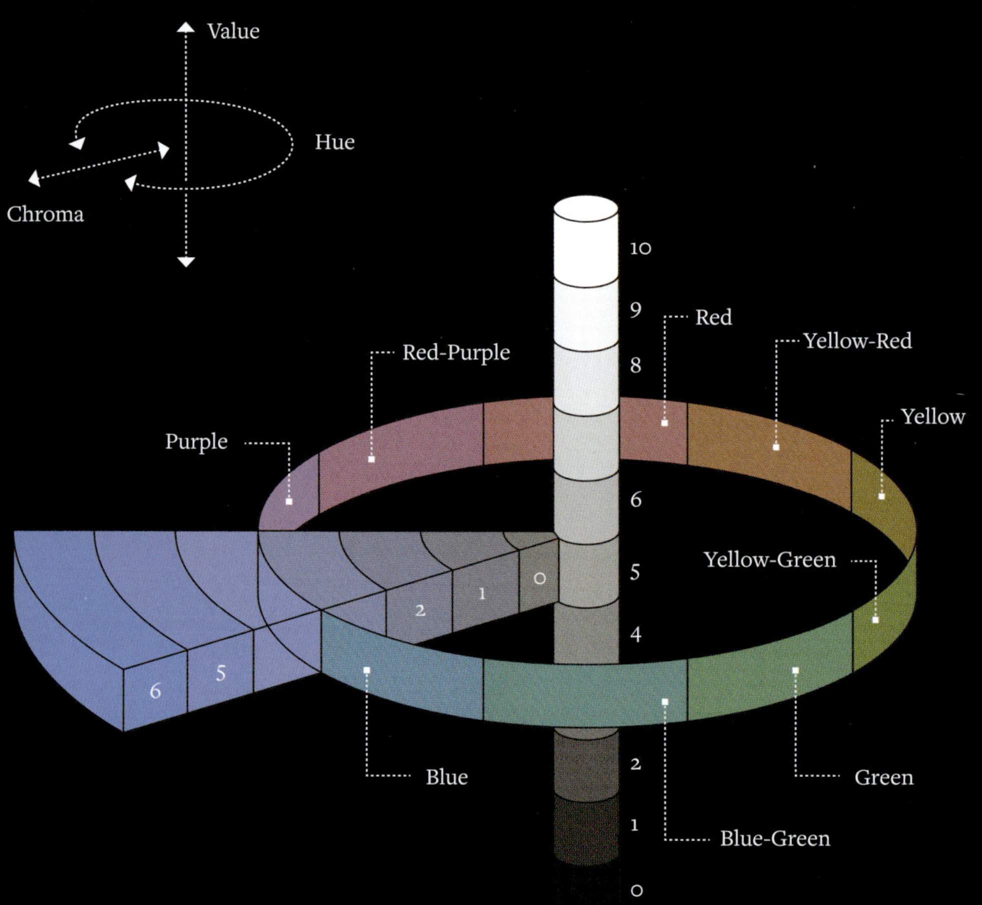

Value
Hue
Chroma
10
9
8
Red
Yellow-Red
Red-Purple
Yellow
Purple
6
5
Yellow-Green
4
2
1
6
5
Blue
Green
2
Blue-Green
1
0

Introduction

The attributes of colour dealt with in this chapter are essential to understanding and working with colour. Hue, value, saturation, temperature and opacity/transparency are all elements that artists should be familiar with, and an understanding of each of them will underpin any successful work in colour.

This chapter, one of the most important in the book, was also probably the one I found hardest to write. Quite apart from the subject matter being challenging, I found myself subconsciously trying to conform the work to a digital or 3D model of colour theory. I would watch a presentation or video on colour theory that would explain that all the centuries of study done in physical colour before the advent of the computer are now wrong, and then I would return to my palette only to discover that paint stubbornly refused to conform to the virtual colour models I so admired.

Virtual colour models can be beautiful and wonderfully useful things. They usually demonstrate three key attributes of colour – hue, saturation and value – and often look something like the diagram opposite. This is the three-dimensional Munsell colour space, but a wide range of other models exist, including the CIE colour spaces (CIELCH, CIELUV, CIELAB and CIECAMO2), the Swedish Natural Colour System (NCS), the Frank Preucil hue circle, RYB colour models, CMY and CMYK models used predominantly in the printing industry, HSL and HSV models used in graphics software and image editing, the Optical Society of America's Uniform Color Scales (OSA-UCS), the Hungarian Coloroid system, Pantone and the German RAL colour matching systems, among many others.

Left The Munsell colour space

All these models can offer you a different insight, but as an artist you should still primarily be guided by what you see in front of you on your palette. The colours we have in paint form have within them their own unique set of physical qualities that, above all others, we would be wise to learn and follow. You can absorb all the information about colour from every source you find and then compare and, if possible, assimilate this into your understanding of paint, but regardless, let paint itself be your guide above all other sources.

So how does colour in paint differ from colour in a virtual environment?

Paint, I would suggest, has more than three 'dimensions', or properties. While most digital colour models show only hue, saturation and value, paint has many other physical attributes that are relevant to the way in which colour is conveyed. You can touch it and form it; it has depth, texture and substance. It can be a liquid, a paste or, when dried, a solid. It can be transparent, semi-transparent or opaque. It is prone to chemical reactions and interactions and its ability to convey colour to the viewer will depend entirely on its environment. To limit a description of colour in paint to three dimensions can subconsciously be limiting to the artist.

The first three sections in this chapter will go into detail on hue, value and saturation. We will then move on to a section about colour temperature, and finally there is a section dealing with opacity and transparency.

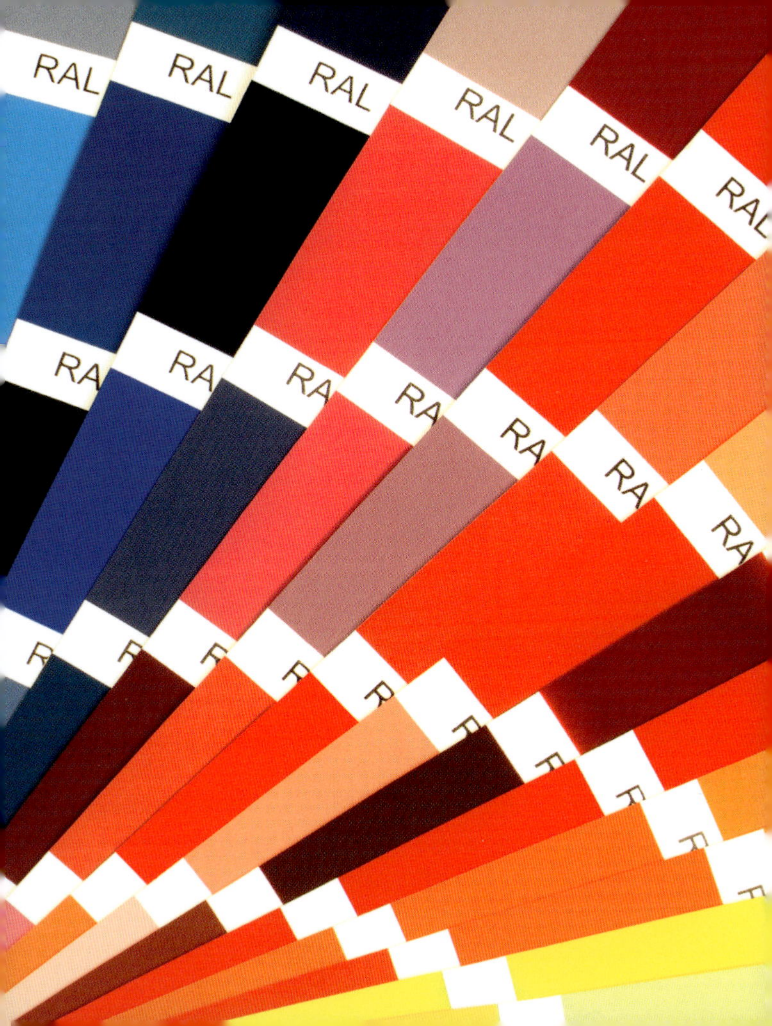

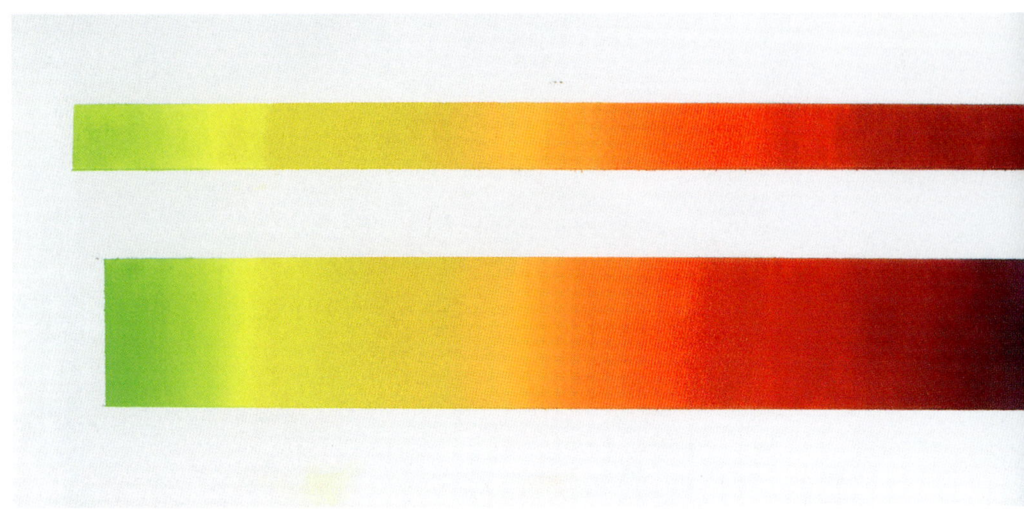

Hue

Hue is the term used to describe the most basic property of a pure colour: its name. It is what differentiates one colour from the next at a very basic level – such as red, yellow, blue and green. The other attributes of colour that we will look at later in this chapter are just extra ways of describing a hue in an altered state. Hue is at the centre.

The International Commission on Illumination, or CIE (for its French name Commission Internationale de l'Éclairage, the international authority on colour and light), describes hue as 'the degree to which a stimulus can be described as similar to or different from stimuli that are described as red, orange, yellow, green, blue, violet'.

When buying or using paint, you may also have noticed that hue can be a way of describing a pigment that is visually almost identical to another, but not the genuine thing. Cadmium red hue, for instance, will be the same 'hue' (colour) as cadmium red genuine, but may not contain any actual cadmium, and other pigment properties found in the original may be different. It is therefore the same colour, but made with different pigment.

The Attributes *of* Colour

Apart from that material-specific usage, when we talk about hue in painting, we mean it is a pure pigment colour, one that hasn't been adjusted by the addition of either tint or shade (that is, added white or black, respectively).

Hues follow the spectrum in a wonderfully predictable pattern which is tremendously helpful to the artist. Sunsets and sunrises, for instance, will follow this orderly pattern of bright yellow, orange, warm red and cool red, and perhaps even purple. A cool light will perhaps start with lemon yellow, green or cyan and transition through neutral blue and then darker warm blue, just as it does on the spectrum. Even colour in the shadows seems to regularly follow this spectrum order.

So often when I'm trying to work out transitional colour patterns for what I'm seeing in nature, I'll refer to the spectrum order of colours, and nine times out of ten they'll provide the answer to what colours I'm seeing or what colour comes next. They are, to quote William Shakespeare, 'an ever-fixed mark', or pattern in this case, which rarely changes and is a continual source of information and reference.

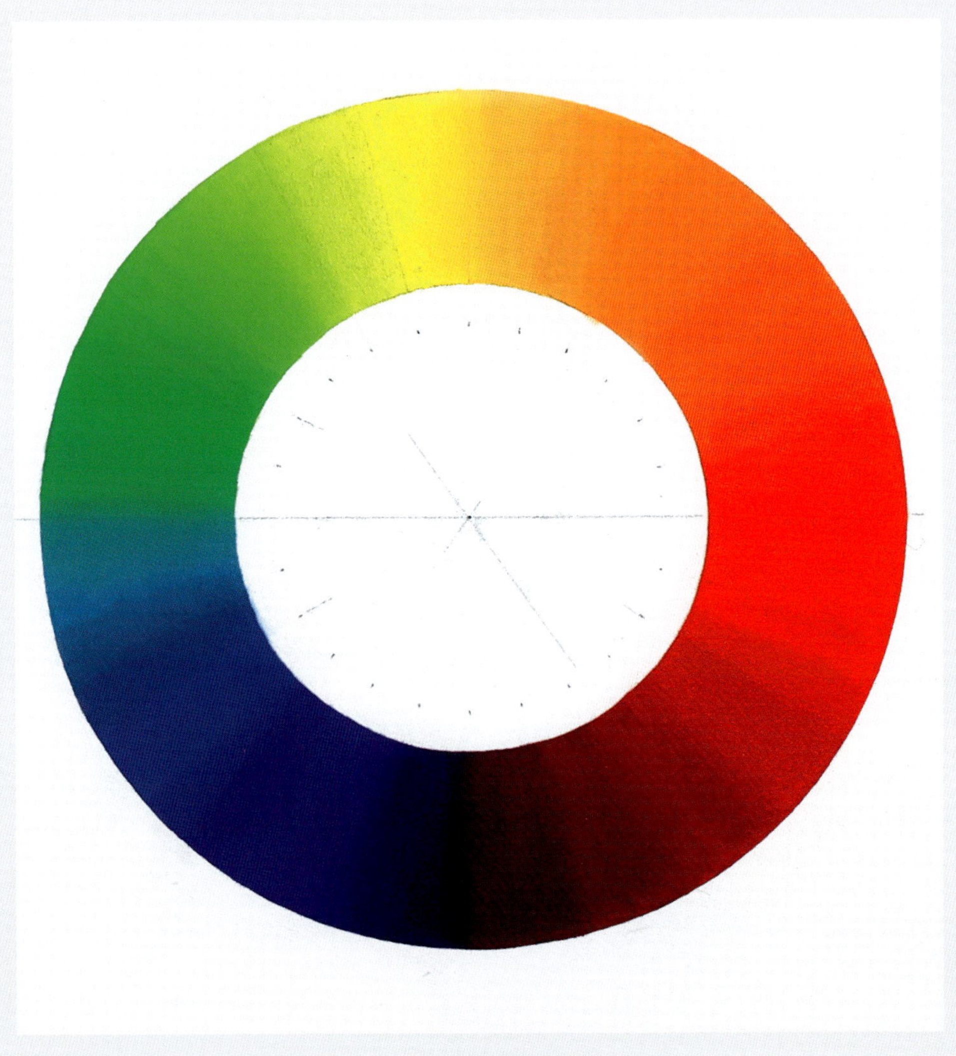

In the chart on pages 30–1, I have portrayed this order or spectrum of hues as a linear strip but, of course, hue is often represented as a circle or wheel (see the diagram opposite).

You might have learnt this order of colours with the acronym ROYGBIV: red, orange, yellow, green, blue, indigo and violet. In the UK, it is known from the mnemonic 'Richard of York gave battle in vain', most likely a reference to the 3rd Duke of York, who died in the Battle of Wakefield in 1460.

Technically, if you're going to have one of each primary and secondary in your spectrum/acronym, it should really be ROYGBP – red (primary), orange (secondary), yellow (primary), green (secondary), blue (primary), purple (secondary) – but that rather ruins the traditional phrase, and my unhallowed hands should probably leave it as it is.

The Newtonian version features two purples (indigo and violet); some other models feature two of each primary and secondary, or three of each primary and secondary, for example. In other popular diagrams, the dimensions of colour are visualised as a ball, and hue is a band around the circumference, a sort of horizontal colour wheel. I sometimes find this to be an unhelpful way to visualise colour, by introducing a three-dimensionality that colour doesn't have in the physical world.

All of this is to say that these charts are always one singular visualisation of the spectrum and can vary depending on the author's emphasis or intent.

Remember that the actual order of spectrum colours is a continuum in real life, and the breaks in our spectrum charts are merely to help us visualise and differentiate the changes in hue.

Hue is inextricably linked to the name of a colour, and if you move along the hue scale from side to side, the name of the colour will change; it will no longer be the colour you started with. For instance, if you start at a hue that we might name 'cool yellow' and move along the scale towards orange, you might stop at a new hue that we could call 'warm yellow', as it contains more of a red influence. The colour can still be broadly described as yellow, but it now needs a new name to differentiate the new hue from the cool yellow you started from.

In this example, we're using temperature as a way of differentiating the colours (warm or cool), but you might equally use other descriptive factors instead. Cool yellow could also be named green-yellow or blue-yellow, if we use colour bias instead of temperature to define the visible difference. It's the same hue, but we're using two different ways to describe it. We might also use relative darkness or light to describe the hue and say that it is a light yellow or dark yellow. Hue is still at the centre, but other qualities are being used to describe a hue which has undergone some alteration.

In some respects, the naming of hues is a little like the Linnaean classification system for naming plants and animals, where we have kingdoms, family, genus and species. In colour, we have broad descriptions for colour families too, such as yellows, greens, blues, purples, reds and oranges. We can then subdivide these broad groups, perhaps into their temperatures, and give names such as warm red or cool red. Or we could subdivide by bias, with yellow-red or blue-red. With a computer model, you can get even more precise and do this by the percentage of component hues and values. So, you can see how a seemingly simple subject can be made more complex, depending upon the degree to which you wish to classify it.

To summarise, hue is how we name the colours on the spectrum and differentiate them from one another. These colours follow a predictable pattern that is useful to us as artists.

In some respects, the naming of hues is a little like the Linnaean classification system for naming plants and animals, where we have kingdoms, family, genus and species.

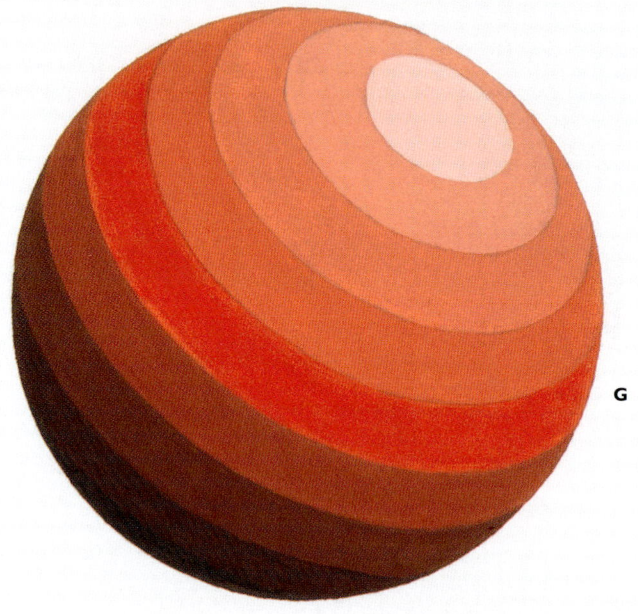

G

0% TONALITY
100% TONALITY

Value

In the context of colour, value refers to relative lightness or darkness. It is the contrast in values that helps us to perceive structure when we look at the world around us, and in painting, value is invaluable for trying to recreate form in what we see. Just look at the room around you and try to imagine what it would look like if all the colours were the same value, none lighter or darker than the next, just a uniform mid-grey tonality. Value is what helps us perceive depth and form; it is what makes the world appear three-dimensional.

From Aristotle (384–322 BCE) to Johann Wolfgang Goethe (1749–1832), the concept of value has always perplexed and fascinated colour theorists and artists. Aristotle believed that colour itself was the *result* of the mixture of light and darkness. We can perhaps have some sympathy with this view when we see how colour can be diminished, or neutralised, by both light and darkness in almost identical ways. The amount of light reflecting from the surface of a colour and the colour of that light can dramatically alter the way we see a thing. Look at a painting from the front and then

the side to see how much the colour and value can change just by changing the angle it's viewed from – and the amount of light that is therefore reflected to you.

Value is perhaps an easier concept to grasp when seen in black and white. In the value scale diagram opposite (below the ball diagram), we have white (the lightest value), black (the darkest value) and a range of percentages of black and white, seen as greys (or tones), in between.

Individual colours have their own intrinsic value as well: yellow is a light-value colour, and purple is a dark-value colour. Within each, however, it is possible to make another colour, and these individual colours can also have their values altered – for instance, both yellow and purple can be made lighter or darker in value – although altering a colour's value will always change its hue or saturation or both.

A colour is at its most vibrant and saturated in the 'Goldilocks Zone' (marked G) in the middle, where light isn't washing it out and darkness isn't dragging it into the gloom, as the classic ball diagram opposite demonstrates.

There are generally three ways in which you can alter the value of any given colour, and they are as follows:

Method 1: Add an adjacent colour from the spectrum

This has the effect of altering the value, but also altering the hue. Adding warm yellow to orange will lighten the value of the orange, but it will also shift the hue sideways along the spectrum scale towards warm yellow. Adding warm red to orange will darken the orange mix and draw it more towards warm red on the spectrum. This may well be a desirable effect in some situations, but it is important to recognise that the colour you started with will no longer be the same.

The Attributes of Colour

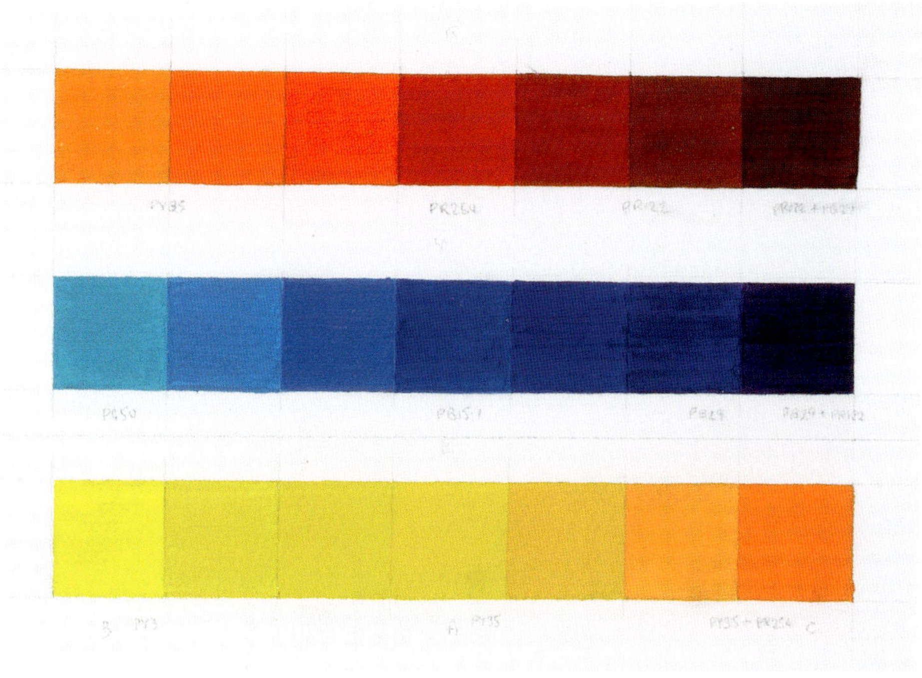

Above Values adjusted by using spectrum-adjacent colours

Method 2: Add a value modifier such as white, grey or black

This will darken or lighten the target colour, but it will also reduce the saturation. The other problem you may face is finding a truly 'colour neutral' white, grey or black to add to your colour. Lightening a colour's value using white or a lighter-value adjacent primary is relatively painless, as white doesn't have a massive colour bias, but what about darkening the value? Black can be especially tricky in this regard, as most blacks have a very strong blue bias. Even white can be visually cool or warm: lead white is warm and titanium white is cool. If you add most pre-made blacks to yellow, they will turn the yellow to green. If it's a warm yellow with a red bias and you want to push it in the opposite direction on the spectrum towards orange and red, the extra blue bias in the black will add to the red present in warm yellow and orange and create a true tertiary colour: yellow + red = orange + blue from the black = brown.

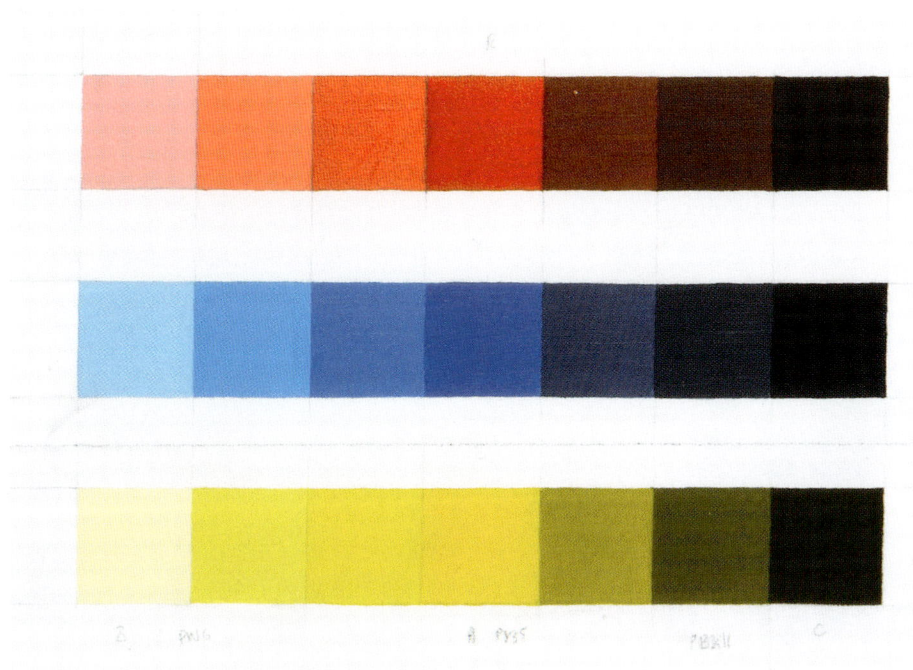

Above Values adjusted by using white and black

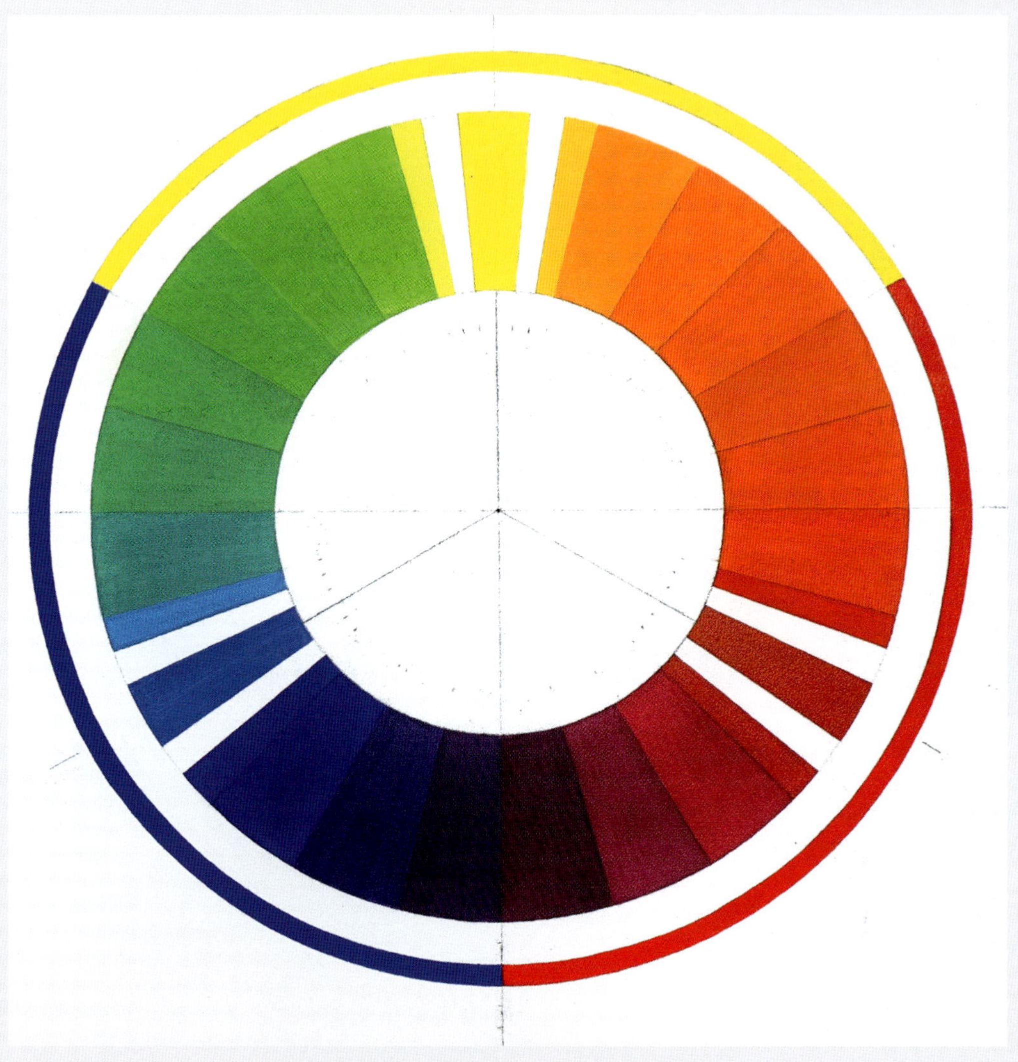

Above Use a colour wheel to find your colour's complementary.

Method 3: Add the colour's complementary colour

This can be a much more reliable way to darken a colour without adversely affecting the hue, and it can achieve the same result as adding a black. The method will theoretically work on nearly any colour, but you will need to know the component colours of your target colour to get it right. To begin, let's see how this applies to the simplest set of colours we have available to us: the primary and secondary colours.

If we take red as an example, adding the two missing primary colours yellow and blue, which together make the complementary green, will usually darken it while neutralising the saturation, but then this is what happens in real life too. Darkness and light both diminish saturation eventually.

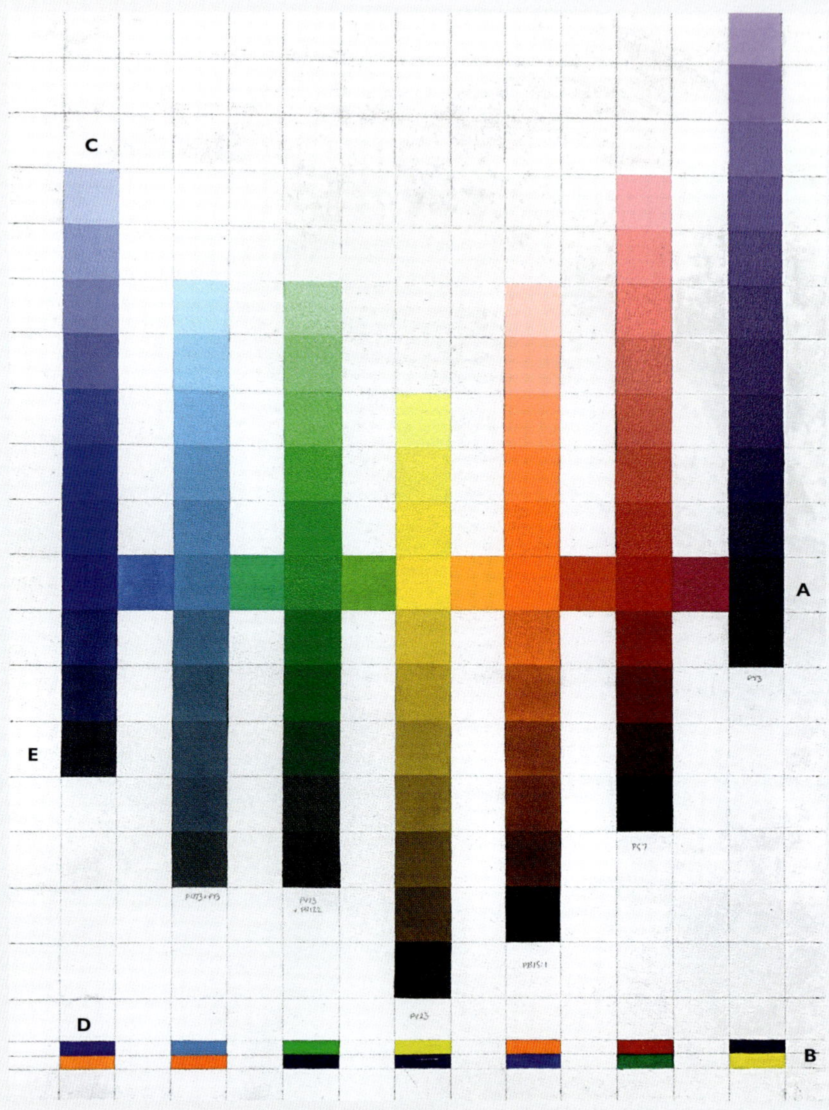
C
A
E
D
B
PV3
PB73+PY3
PY3 + PR122
PY23
PBr5:1
PG7

In the chart opposite, the horizontal bar (A) represents the order of hues as we've seen in the previous section (see page 31). The vertical bars are some of the hues that I've darkened and lightened. If they're above the horizontal bar, I've incrementally added white to the colour. If the colour is below the horizontal bar, I've slowly added that colour's complementary colour to darken the target colour. At the base of the diagram, I've also painted the colours used as two coloured bars (B): the coloured bar above is the colour from the horizontal 'hue' strip (A), and the one below is the colour used to neutralise that colour and darken it to achieve black, its complementary colour.

Let's take the colour on the left (C) as our first example. Before painting each strip, I took my target colour (in this case, a warm blue) and added the missing primaries (mixed as secondary – in this instance, orange (D)). The initial result was a little too purple when I mixed it, which indicated that the orange I was adding was too red (remember, warm blue contains a red bias). I therefore added a little more yellow to the orange until it mixed a

black (E) instead of a deep purple. If the mixed colour had been greener, that would have indicated not enough red and too much yellow, in which case I would have added a little red.

This process does take some practice, but once you tune into which of the three primaries is missing to make the mix neutral, and bear in mind a colour's biases, it will become second nature. After all, you're only ever mixing three colours. All you need to do is work out the correct ratios.

The second colour from the left is a cool blue (cyan), which contains a yellow bias, so this required a slightly redder orange to achieve neutrality. It's difficult to tell from the colour strips at the base of the diagram, but the orange on the left is much more yellow in nature than the one on the right. I've added this cool blue (cyan) to the chart, as it's a good visual demonstration of just how important the darkness and opacity of your blue is to the resultant black mixes. Cyan is somewhere in the mid-to-lighter end of the value scale, plus many shop-bought cyans contain white, so the neutral colour this will create when orange is added is more grey than black. In these mixes, the value and transparency or opacity of the blue used is usually responsible for how dark we can make the neutral/black, as blue is the dominant quantity in any black mix.

The green strip is an interesting one because it was mixed using phthalocyanine blue (PB15) and lemon yellow (PY3), but there were such tiny amounts of blue needed for the green mix that instead of adding just red (the missing of the three primaries), I needed to add a very red purple (for the extra blue), made from magenta (PR122) and dioxazine purple (PV23). This meant that because the added colour was very dark, the resulting black was dark too, unlike the cyan.

The cyan could have been darkened further, but this would have needed the addition of a dark, more transparent blue, such as phthalocyanine blue (PB15:1 or PB15:3), instead of the opaque cyan that I was using.

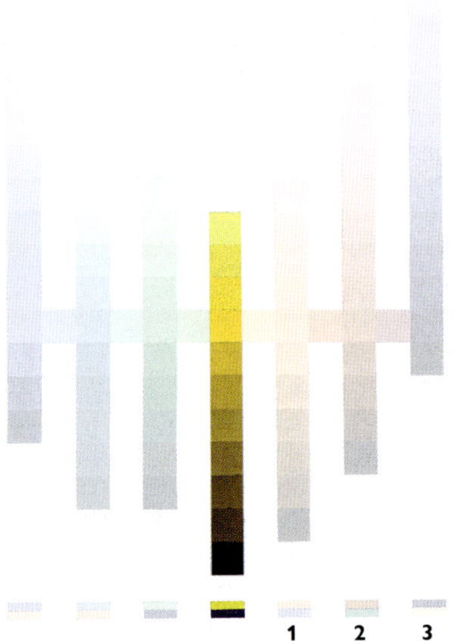

The central yellow strip is lemon yellow (PY3) with a touch of cadmium yellow (PY35) to make it a little more neutral. To this I've simply added dioxazine purple (PV23). The orange strip (1) has had phthalocyanine blue (PB15) added. The red strip (2) has had phthalocyanine green (PG7) added, which makes a superb black and value modifier in this instance, almost certainly due to the inherent transparent darkness of phthalocyanine green. Lastly, the purple strip (3) is the reverse of the yellow strip, with lemon yellow (PY3) being added to purple instead of the other way around. Some of these mixes were quite straightforward while others needed a lot more 'tuning' to get just right.

The Attributes *of* Colour

What's interesting about this chart is the neat value curve it creates. What you may notice is that the lightest colour (yellow) has the greatest capacity for being made darker – its tonal range – and the darkest colour (purple) has the greatest capacity for being made lighter in value – its tinting range. Yellow needs the darkest colour (purple) to become darker and eventually become black, and purple needs the lightest colour (yellow) to achieve black. They couldn't be farther away from one another on the spectrum, or more different in value, and yet they both need one another to achieve neutrality and create black in a curious symmetry.

Interestingly, there seems to be a strong correlation between the value and position on the spectrum of the other pairs too. If you look at the colours the strips are mixed from (at the bottom of the chart), the value of the top colours gets lighter on either side of yellow, and on the bottom, they start dark and get lighter on either side of purple. On the top set of colours, we have the natural order of the spectrum and on the bottom a sort of mirror of those colours.

Also, of course, if you work out the darkest value for your colours using this mixing method, the resulting black will provide you with a neutral base for mixing a range of greys by adding white. These could be added to your target colour without altering the hue; therefore, they are true neutrals. Instead of guessing what shade or hue of grey to add, you could confidently add a grey that you know matches the colour you are trying to modify.

This is why traditional charts have always bothered me. They showed me what a colour should look like with a grey added but gave no clue how to achieve that colour. Altering the value by adding grey on a computer model is easy, but in practice and with paint, this is rarely an easy task. With the method we've just discussed, you now know you will be able to find a match for the colour you are modifying and can make a reliable range of tints and tones from it without adversely altering the hue.

The diagram opposite shows a wheel of spectrum colours in order, and the complementary colours needed to neutralise them and create black, or near black. This chart was a real headache to produce but yielded some interesting results. I hope it will be useful when it comes to your own experiments with changing the values of colours in paint.

What is my colour's complementary?

When doing this exercise, ask yourself questions such as:

Is there a warm or cool colour bias in my primary colours that I need to account for in their complementary?

Do I need to adjust the ratios of the primary colours I'm mixing?

Can I use a premixed secondary colour?

In theory, this principle is simple. However, in practice, it takes a very specific pairing to create black. For instance, if you add a purple to a yellow that hasn't got the balance just right, you might make a dark greenish or orangey colour that isn't quite black. The ratios need to be quite specific for the combinations to cancel out all visible colour and create black.

So, what's the point? Well, if you can locate exactly which hue you need to cancel out your target colour, you can create a black that will darken your colour without influencing its hue. This is tremendously useful if you wish to retain the hue but want to gradually darken it. In terms of colour dimensions, this would allow you to darken straight down without moving sideways along the hue scale.

The Attributes *of* Colour

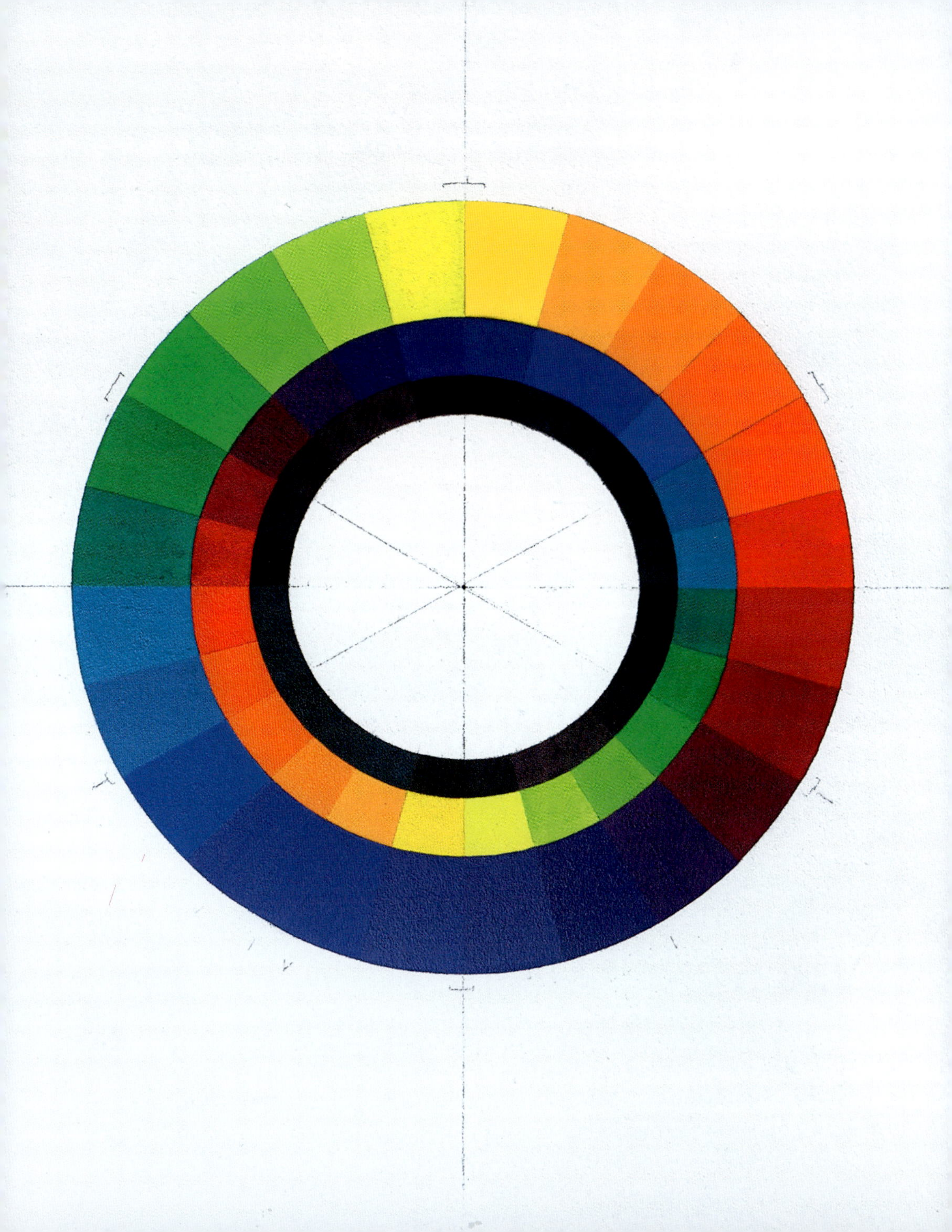

Saturation

Loosely defined as a colour's intensity, this attribute has many different names that are almost synonymous, and they can each offer us some insight into exactly what we mean by it. The differences are subtle but important.

Chroma is the term that is most ubiquitously used in the fine art world. Popularised by A.H. Munsell (1858–1918), it is the Greek word for colour, which has always struck me as a little confusing, as you could argue that it should be assigned to hue instead.

Purity is also often used as an alternative term, as a colour unaltered by black, white, grey or another colour could be said to be pure. But I feel this also brings in the potential for confusion, as pure implies being free from any other influencing factor, including hue bias or value.

For paint, vibrancy has always struck me as a nice option to describe how visually arresting a colour is. A colour at full vibrancy almost seems to oscillate visually. Vibrant colours, such as cadmium red (PR108) and ultramarine blue (PB29), are so full of energy, they are almost uncomfortable to look at for long.

Vibrant colours, such as cadmium red (PR108) and ultramarine blue (PB29), are so full of energy, they are almost uncomfortable to look at for long.

     The Attributes *of* Colour

Of all the synonyms used for this attribute, saturation is the one I feel is most useful for our purposes here because it is descriptively accurate. If you're familiar with virtual colour models, digital modelling or photo manipulation applications, for example, I expect you're already familiar with the term saturation. My only slight reservation when applying this to paint is that a pigment can be fully saturated with pure colour and yet still not have the intensity the term implies.

Ultramarine blue (PB29), for instance, only hits peak saturation when it's spread thinly over a white surface or is diluted slightly by white. It's saturated with pure colour, but it needs help to be seen at its full potential. It's still an issue of light, as in a virtual model, but I think the distinction in the physical world of paint is a significant one.

In this section, I will use saturation and vibrancy interchangeably to refer to this colour attribute.

Simply put, saturation concerns how colourful – or 'colour-full' – a colour is. High saturation refers to a colour that is very vibrant or strong, whereas low saturation refers to a colour that tends towards being dull or grey.

Light and darkness exert the same power over a colour's vibrancy, oddly mirroring one another on either side of peak saturation. Light diminishes saturation on one side in the same way that darkness diminishes saturation on the other. Saturation is at its peak where colour is balanced between too much light or too much darkness.

Value and saturation are intrinsically linked to one another; reduce or increase value and saturation will also be affected. But while value can exist in an achromatic (uncoloured or greyscale) form, and be represented as such, saturation must have value.

Try to picture a colour's saturation without value. If you can think of anything at all, you might think of a colour in a pure state as you would see it on the spectrum, but even these pure colours have their own value. Even colours at peak saturation, unaffected by excess or insufficient light, have an inherent value that differentiates them from one another.

When it comes to paint, saturation can be altered in a variety of ways.

One of the most common methods is to add a white, premixed grey or black to a colour. This method works but involves some forethought about how much or how little of the additional black, white or grey is needed. When you're mixing paint there are few, if any, clear ways to measure ratios. This is predominantly done by eye and is therefore subjective when mixing up a colour or a grey. For example, what exactly does 30% grey look like in terms of value? If you do manage to determine this – probably by comparing it to a printed strip – how much volume of that grey do you then add to your colour?

Artists must also be careful of colour bias. Grey almost always has a colour bias, and that bias is usually blue. Yellow will be particularly sensitive to this bias and the resultant mixes can vary wildly depending on the black you use in your grey mix.

In the diagram opposite, I've chosen lemon yellow (PY3) and incrementally added different greys to it, to illustrate how the hue as well as the value changes when you use similar greys, but with differing hue biases.

As you can see, the popular admixture of value using grey can be problematic, even if this method can produce some truly wonderful colours and is a solid method to utilise for adjusting saturation.

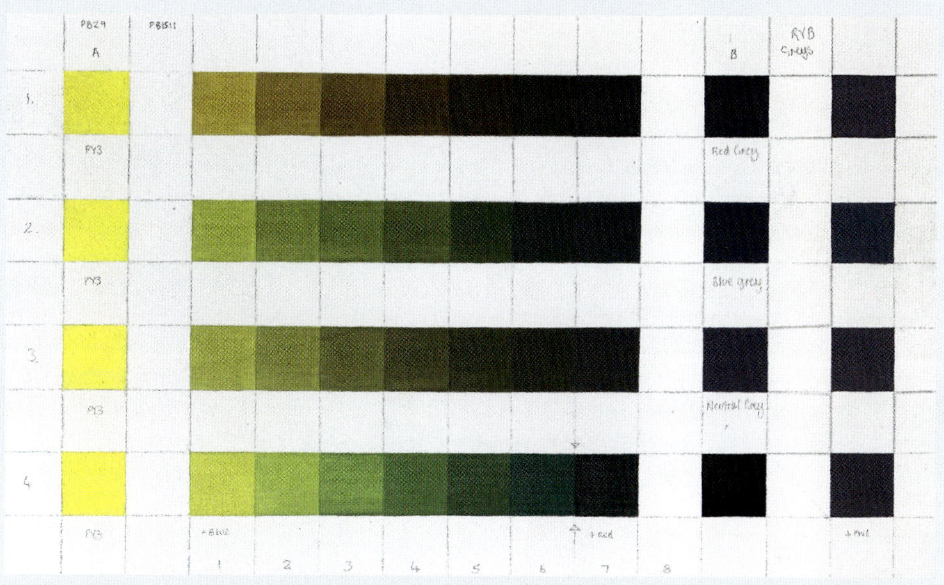

PB29
PB15:1
A
B
RYB greys
1.
PY3
Red Grey
2.
PY3
Blue grey
3.
PY3
Neutral grey
4
PY3
+ Blue
+ Red
+ Wht
1   2   3   4   5   6   7   8

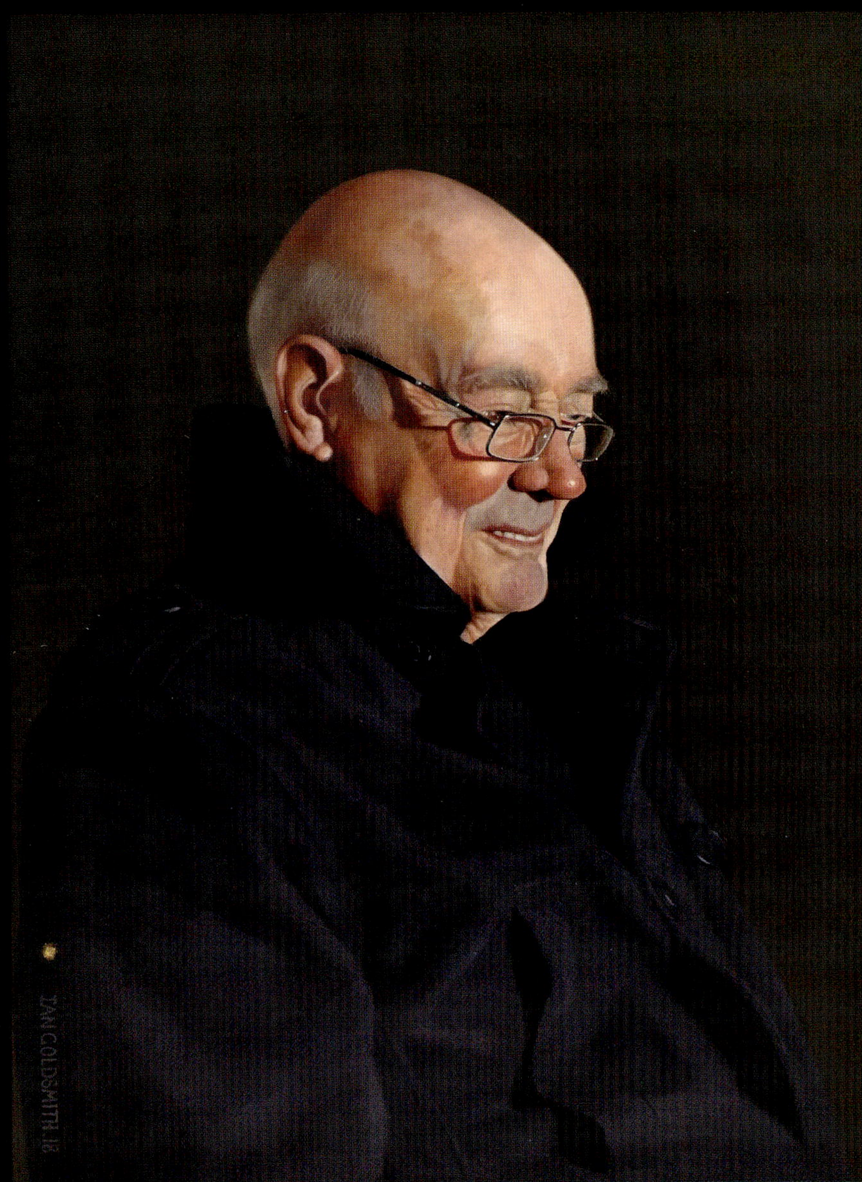

IAN GOLDSMITH. 18

Another method used to adjust saturation is to apply a transparent colour over a toned surface. This method has been utilised for centuries and is traditionally used in conjunction with 'grisaille'. Grisaille is from *gris* – the French word for grey – and is a method of painting an image in black and white, or a neutral colour capable of producing a wide range of tints and tones. Grisaille is commonly used as a monochrome underpainting, over which is applied a glaze, or glazes, of transparent colour. In this way, the grisaille layer provides the tonal structure of the image, and the glaze provides the colour to its tints and tones, a bit like looking at a black-and-white photograph through a piece of coloured glass or plastic.

Grisaille and glazing work hand in hand. With grisaille, you can control the value of the colour by the amount of available light beneath the thin film of paint used over it.

This method has issues too, of course. With glazing, you must allow time for the base coat of grey to dry before you can safely apply the glaze over it. Thankfully, the grisaille layer is commonly painted in umber (burnt umber or raw umber) mixed with white. The umbers oxidise – and therefore dry – much more quickly than most other colours. However, umber is brown and can dramatically affect the colour applied over it. A neutral grey mixed with black and a warm umber will help with the drying time and the colour bias. Being an iron oxide, Mars black (PBk11) will dry the fastest of the blacks, but any black will benefit from the increased oxidation rates of an added umber.

I used this method in a portrait of my father, shown opposite, where I had worked out the values in the underpainting first. In this case, I didn't underpaint in true grisaille, with grey, but in shades of blue on the coat. I was struggling to achieve a satisfactory rich navy-blue colour in the coat, and a transparent layer of dark blue over a previous layer of colour allowed the structure of the underpainting to show through in value, while the glaze produced the rich hue I was looking for by intensifying the saturation of the underpainting.

Lastly, we have the admixture of a complementary colour to your target colour. With this method you identify the true complementary colour of your target colour and then add this colour to the target colour to modify and diminish saturation without altering hue. You can do this either by adding the colour directly, or by mixing the complementary colour with the target colour to achieve black, and then add white to this mix to create your range of greys. The latter method is a little more complicated, but it is very reliable once you get the hang of the process. You can find out more information about adding complementary colours in the section on Value (see page 36).

Right Here, a series of identical tonal strips have been glazed over with pure colours. This diagram is a good example of the unpredictability of working with paint: you can see where some paint has bled through under the tape at the edges!

The Attributes *of* Colour

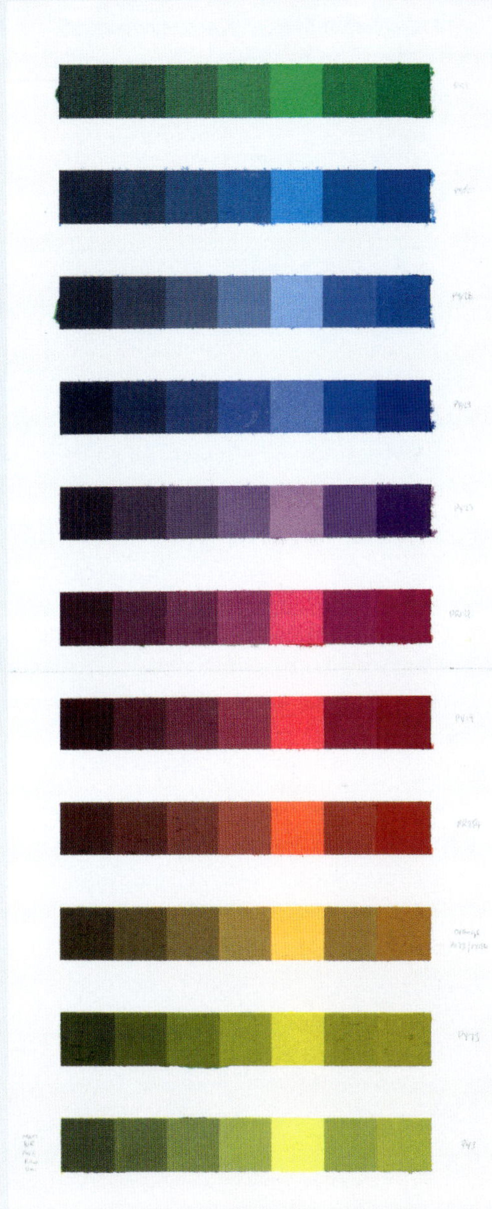

Any discussion about saturation in paint colour needs to touch on transparency and opacity, areas that are largely alien to virtual colour modellers but are only too real to those of us that use paint. In digital simulations of any given colour, its peak saturation is easily displayed on the screen, as it's only a matter of balancing the lightness and darkness of the digital image. In paint, a three-dimensional substance, things aren't quite so simple.

Let's take a colour likely to be familiar to you as an example: ultramarine blue (PB29). When you squeeze this paint out of the tube, it's generally very dark. But it's also transparent, so when it's thin – where light can shine through it and reflect from the, usually white, painting surface underneath – it can look much lighter in value. So, to display ultramarine blue at its peak saturation, you are faced with two options: either to spread it very thinly over a white surface as a glaze and use its

transparency to help you see it better, or to add white to the dark paint and sensitively mix it into the colour to lighten it and therefore make the saturation increasingly intense

The problem with dark transparent colours, such as ultramarine blue, is that it's difficult to control the intensity (saturation) of the colour. The most popular way to do this is to add white. In fact, on some of the diagrams in this book, I've had to add white to make these dark transparent colours visible to the camera. At other times, I've painted the colour very thinly over a white surface, but it hasn't always been easy to display these colours in varying values without sometimes compromising a colour's saturation to make it more visible.

It's not all bad news though. If done carefully, white added to many of these dark transparent colours can produce some truly intense and wonderful hues. There is a sweet spot to be found, where just enough white has been added to bring the colour out of the shadows, but not enough to wash it out and deaden it, which can bring a true vibrancy to these colours. Colours such as magenta (PR122), ultramarine blue (PB29), phthalocyanine blue (PB15:1) and phthalocyanine green (PG7), for instance, can be mixed with white to create incredibly intense colours full of saturation. They can also be used very effectively as glazes.

So, saturation in paint is affected by another 'dimension' that doesn't affect it in many virtual simulations: transparency and opacity. Even printed reference works that display degrees of a colour's saturation aren't really playing fair, as the printing process used to recreate these computer-generated colours doesn't recreate colour in the same way you will on your palette or on your canvas with paint.

We'll discuss transparency and opacity further on page 76.

EXPERIMENTING WITH DIFFERENT METHODS OF ALTERING SATURATION

In this experiment, I painted a strip of 11 tonal gradients using Mars black (PBk11) and titanium white (PW6) at the bottom of the diagram on the opposite page, and then I used this strip as a comparison reference, to illustrate ways to diminish saturation.

The same colour is used for each set of three strips, but they employ different painting methods. The top strip of each set, labelled 'A', has a transparent colour layer painted over grey squares – like those in the reference strip at the bottom of the diagram – after the paint has dried. This glazed strip illustrates how transparent paint can be illuminated from underneath by light reflecting from the prepainted surface and back through the film of coloured paint on top. As the amount of available reflected light from underneath the glaze diminishes, so does the amount of visible colour, and therefore the saturation.

The glaze was made from oil paint mixed with oil until it was a creamy consistency. This was painted on roughly, and then smoothed and brushed out with a clean, dry, synthetic wash-type brush to remove brush marks. It's much the same principle as a 'wash' that you might use with a water-based paint, just a little more labour-intensive. It's important to ensure that the paint you glaze over is very dry, as the thinned paint in the glaze can reactivate the paint in the previous layer and make quite a mess.

The next strip down, 'B' on the diagram, has had the same colour as 'A' mixed directly into the corresponding tint or tone of grey paint before it was applied. With this strip, we get to see what the colour looks like when it's mixed into grey the Munsell way: this is grey/value and colour mixed together, and the saturation is diminished by the addition of value in the form of paint. As you can see, this makes some very attractive colours indeed. Most of the colours we see around us are muted like those yielded by this method.

 The Attributes *of Colour*

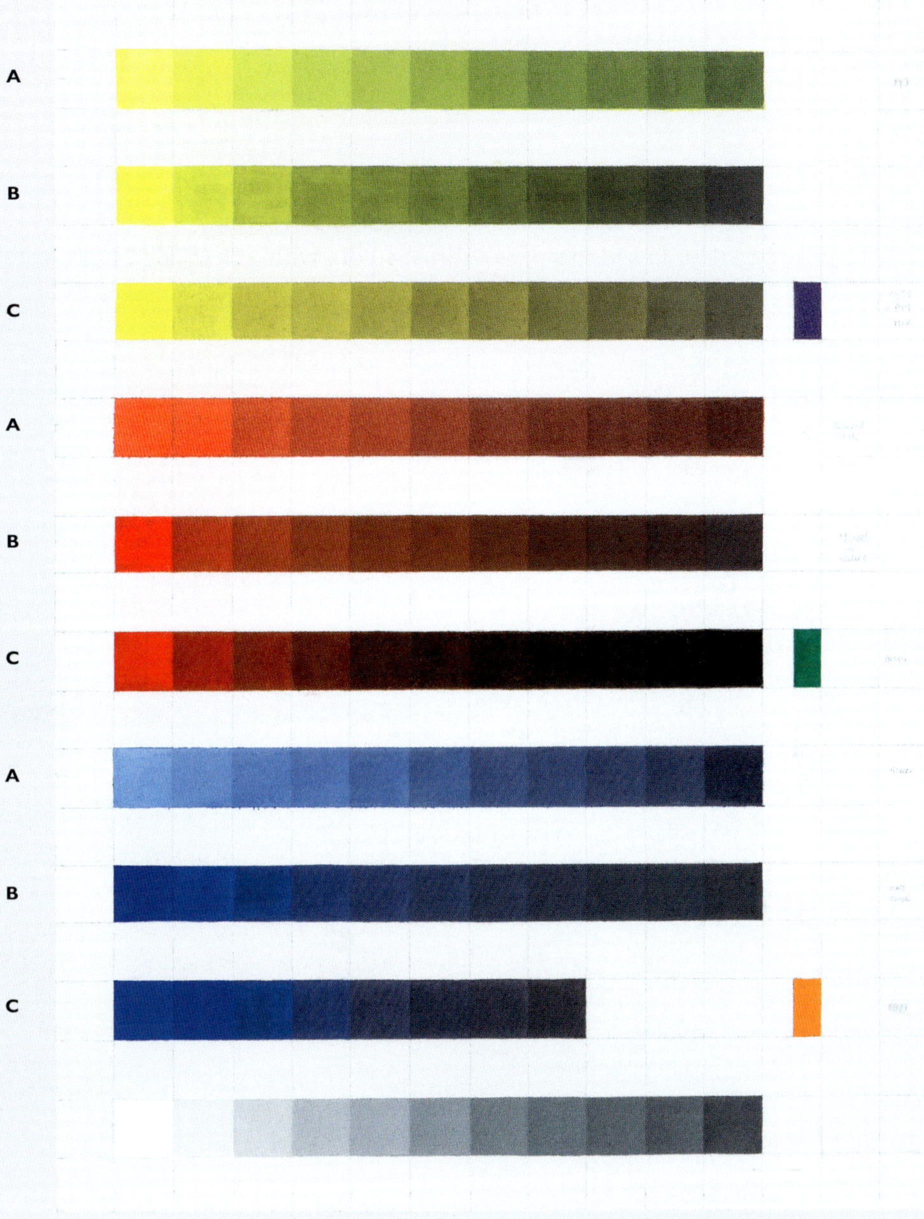

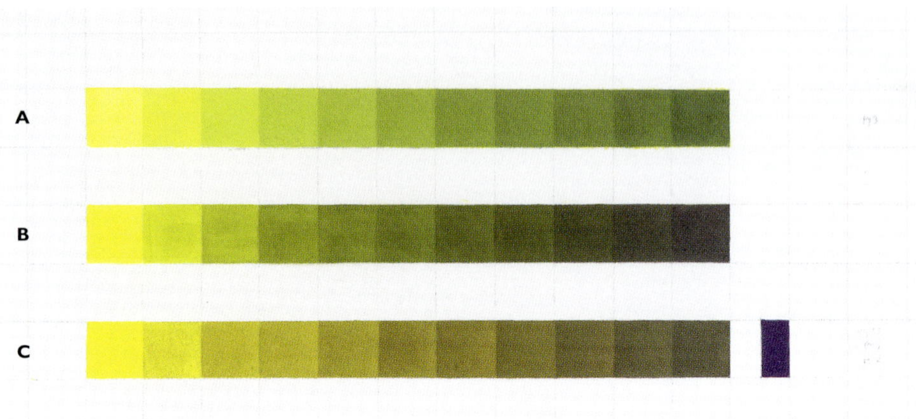

Although this method produces some great results, it is hampered by some intrinsic difficulties. The first is that, as we have seen, grey is rarely neutral. Finding a black to mix with that doesn't have a strong blue bias isn't always easy. In this case, I've used Mars black (PBk11) and it does a pretty good job, but with most blacks you are primarily adding blue to the mix, and this will shift the colour along the hue scale. That might be okay with certain colours, but undesirable with others.

The other issue, as I've mentioned, is the ratios. With a computer model, altering values is just a matter of moving a virtual slider, but what does a percentage of grey look like as paint on your palette? Let's say you have mixed the value of grey you wish to use, and you have the colour you wish to combine it with – what ratios of grey to colour do you use? Depending on the ratios you use of either, you will experience very different results, and a whole host of variations in between. Too little colour and too much grey and you have a muted mix; too little grey and too much colour and you have a very vibrant mix. This isn't to say this isn't a great method for muting colour and diminishing saturation, because

The Attributes *of* Colour

it is, it just takes a lot of practice and experience to master.

So, what about the results? Well, after a *lot* of mixing and comparing I've hopefully produced a strip that demonstrates a comparison using the Munsell method (for want of a better term) to match the value and saturation to the other corresponding tonal gradient strips.

With the final strip, 'C' on the diagram, I've taken the target colour (in this case, yellow, red or blue) and identified the matching complementary colour by adding it to the target colour, and then I've adjusted the

complementary colour until the mix produces black or grey. There are only two colours in your complementary set, so all you need to do is determine how much of each component colour of your complementary is needed to produce a hue that, when added to your primary, will cancel out visible colour and produce black, or something very close to it. It takes practice, but it's something worth investing your time in. Once you have your matched complementary, you just incrementally add it to your primary (or vice versa) to diminish the saturation.

With the yellow strip, I predominantly used lemon yellow (PY3), but I borrowed a little opacity by adding a touch of cadmium lemon yellow (PY35). The PY3 on its own produces a better black when mixed with the purple, but a mix of all transparent colours is very difficult to brush out neatly. I felt the hue with this strip was much freer from bias than either the glazed or the grey admixture methods. Strip B in the lemon-yellow section used the darkest grey from the example strip as an additive to the yellow, which is also why this strip is a little darker.

The red strip C used a red similar
to cadmium red in opacity, pyrrole red
(PR254), mixed with phthalocyanine
green (PG7). In this case, the opacity
of the red mixed beautifully with
the transparent green and made it
a relative joy to work with. Plus, the
green was a perfect match for the
warm red and no adjusting of hue
in the green was needed.

With the blue strip C, I used a
transparent blue, ultramarine (PB29),
and mixed it with a little titanium
white (PW6) to create a lighter, more
visible blue than PB29 straight from
the tube, by borrowing some opacity
from the white. I then added an orange
mix that I had to 'tune' to make it work
for this blue, which I did by adjusting
the quantities of red and yellow. With
these mixes, you add a warm colour
to a cool one and vice versa, so as
ultramarine is a warm blue I needed
a cool orange – that is, one with more
of the component colour that makes
blue cool, which is yellow.

**The value of the hue
plays an important
part in these mixes.**

The Attributes of Colour

The interesting thing about altering value using the complementary method is that although some of the value changes are what you might expect – for instance, adding dark purple to yellow makes it darker – some are not. If you look at the blue strip, I've added what looks like a lighter-value orange to the blue and yet the value gradient has got incrementally darker. Likewise with the red, neither red nor green look anywhere near as dark as the black they created and yet the red and green together yield this result.

It does need to be pointed out that transparency in one or more of the key component colours plays a big part. One or both colours you combine seem to need to be transparent and the best blacks come from combinations of transparent or semi-transparent colours. Too much opacity, particularly in the lighter-value colours, and the results will rarely achieve a good black.

Also worthy of note is the range of values available. I've tried to match the range of values to the example tonal strip at the base of the diagram, but the blue being darker has fewer tonal increments available to it in comparison to yellow, which has too many to fit on the chart. A warm red, such as pyrrole (PR254), for instance, is somewhat mid-tonal, so it has fewer tonal increments than yellow, which is very close to white in value, but more than a dark blue, such as ultramarine (PR29) or phthalocyanine (PB15:1). So, the value of the hue also plays an important part.

Temperature

When we talk about colour temperature as artists, we don't mean the measurable phenomena of the transfer of energy that science classifies as heat. We mean the psychological effect produced in our minds when we see a colour and associate it with a sense of temperature. As a rule, when we see colours in the red or blue range of hues, they evoke in most of us feelings of warmth or coolness respectively.

It is typical to divide the colour spectrum into two neat hemispheres – cool and warm – as per the two diagrams opposite.

If you divide the colour wheel into two halves, with the warm half starting at yellow and ending at purple, and the cool half starting at green and ending at violet, you can see that a spectrum that incorporates more hues can still be divided the same way, and this works well as a general understanding of the two perceived temperature zones.

Experiments have demonstrated a difference of five to seven degrees in the subjective feeling of heat or cold between a work-room painted in blue-green and painted in red-orange. That is, in the blue-green room the occupants felt that 59°F [15°C] was cold, whereas in the red-orange room they did not feel cold until the temperature fell to 52°F [11°C].

Johannes Itten, *The Elements of Color*

The Attributes *of* Colour

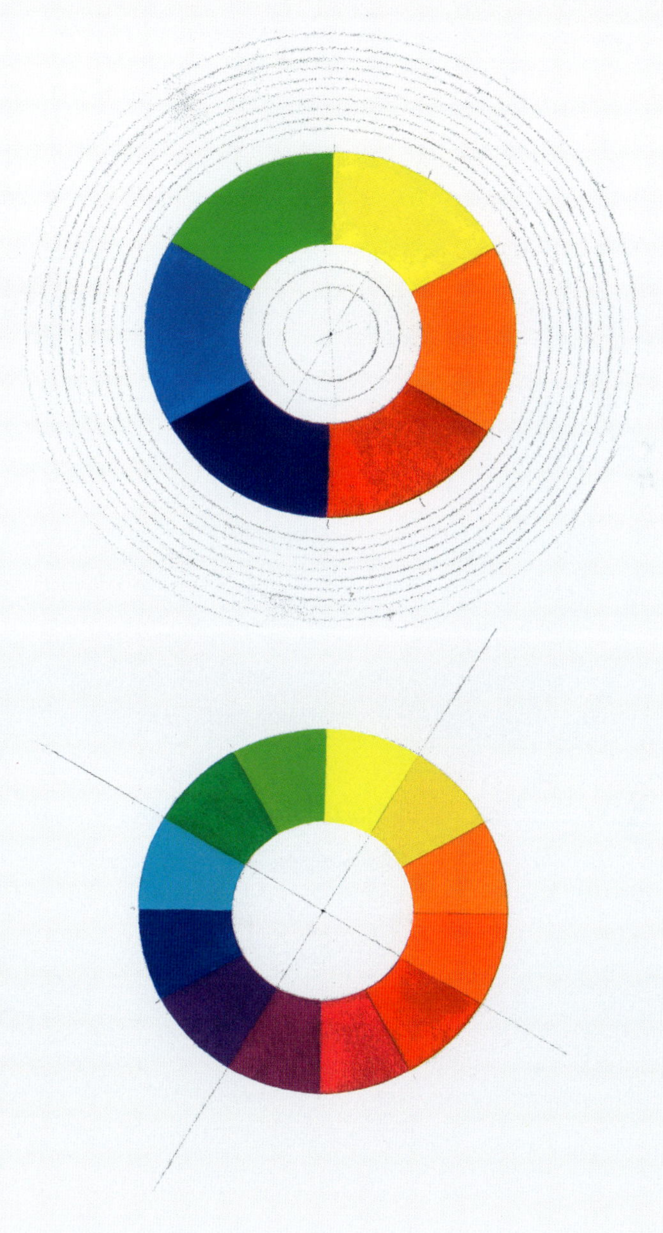

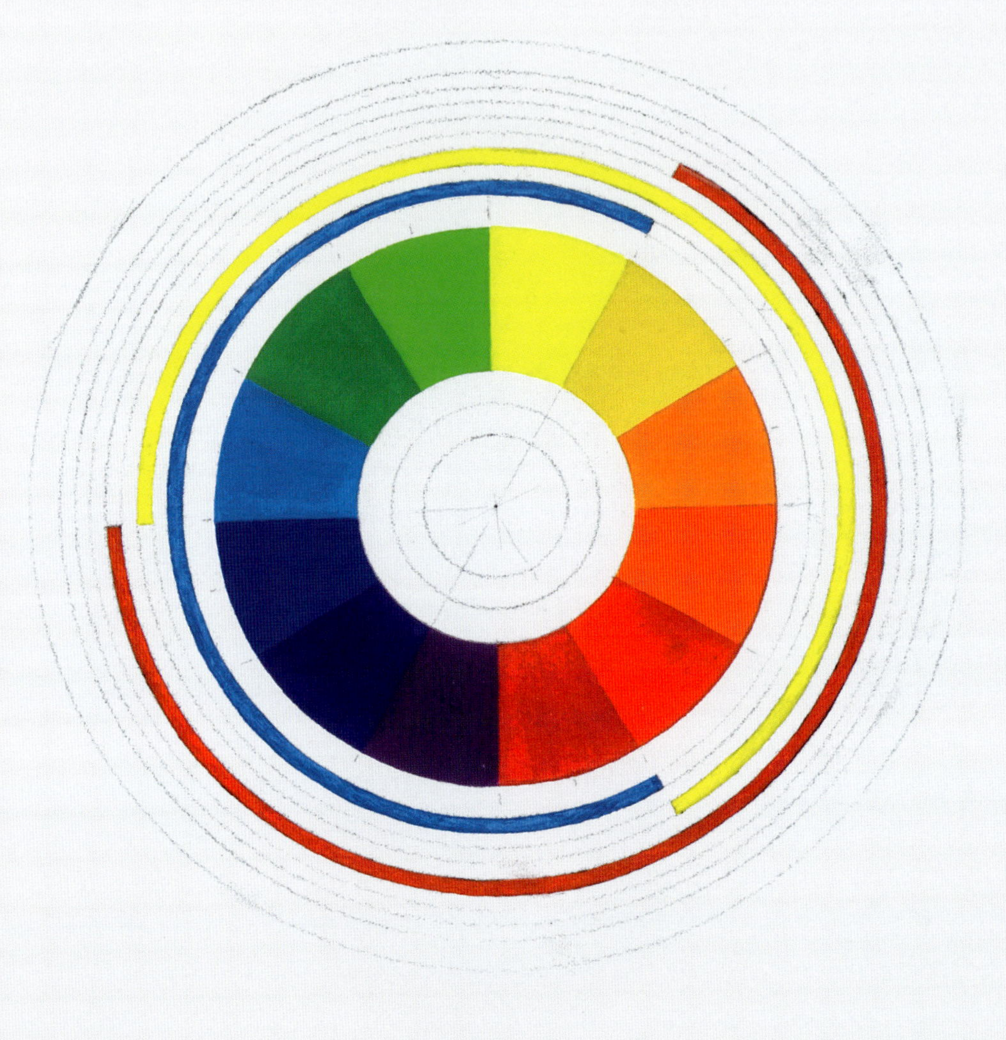

Can we put our finger on what gives each of these colours their associated temperatures? As we have already seen, each colour carries elements of another colour, and that bias (or overtone) can be said to be responsible for the perceived temperature in that colour.

If you look at the diagram opposite, I've added a few extra rings to the temperature wheel. These rings show the extent of the colour influence of the three primaries within the spectrum colours. The range of colours each outer ring encompasses could be said to include some of the colour, or a bias, of that ring. The yellow ring, for instance, encompasses cool blue, through green, yellow, orange and into warm red. These colours could be said to display an influence of yellow within them. Likewise for the colours captured by the red or blue rings. The red ring shows the colours displaying a red influence and the blue ring shows the colours containing a blue influence.

You can check this by applying the adjacent colour mixing principle (see page 39), as cool yellow will mix with cool blue to create the range of greens in between them on the spectrum. Likewise, warm yellow when mixed with warm red will create the corresponding pure range of orange hues found between them on the spectrum. The purity of these mixes indicates the very close relationship between these hues.

It can be said that blue is the key factor (as shown by the colours in the blue ring) in determining if a colour is 'cool' or not, as it covers cool red through to cool yellow. Equally, red could be said to determine visual warmth, as it covers warm blue through to warm yellow. Theoretically, there should also be a neutral version of each primary that is not influenced by any other primary. This is illustrated in the diagram opposite.

In paint, however, this neutrality is a bit like finding the proverbial unicorn, and every primary I've ever used displays a temperature bias.

What you will also notice with these three rings is the influence of yellow, and this is where the clearly defined temperature idea falls apart, or at least adds another factor worth considering. Yellow, it seems, is the defining influence: a blue containing a yellow bias is said to be a cool blue, but yellow is also what defines a red as warm.

Green could be said to be cool when the majority bias is blue, and orange could be said to be warm when the greater influence within it is red, but if we move past the theoretical neutral point of green or orange and move in the other direction, the primary influence is yellow. This suggests that yellow is a sort of neutral zone on the spectrum. While you still might say that orange is warm – it does contain red, after all – and green cool because it contains blue, there is a theoretical point in each where if the influence of yellow is greater than the influence of either red or blue, it could be said they are moving towards temperature neutrality, the epicentre of which must surely be found between cool yellow and warm yellow, in the neutral zone.

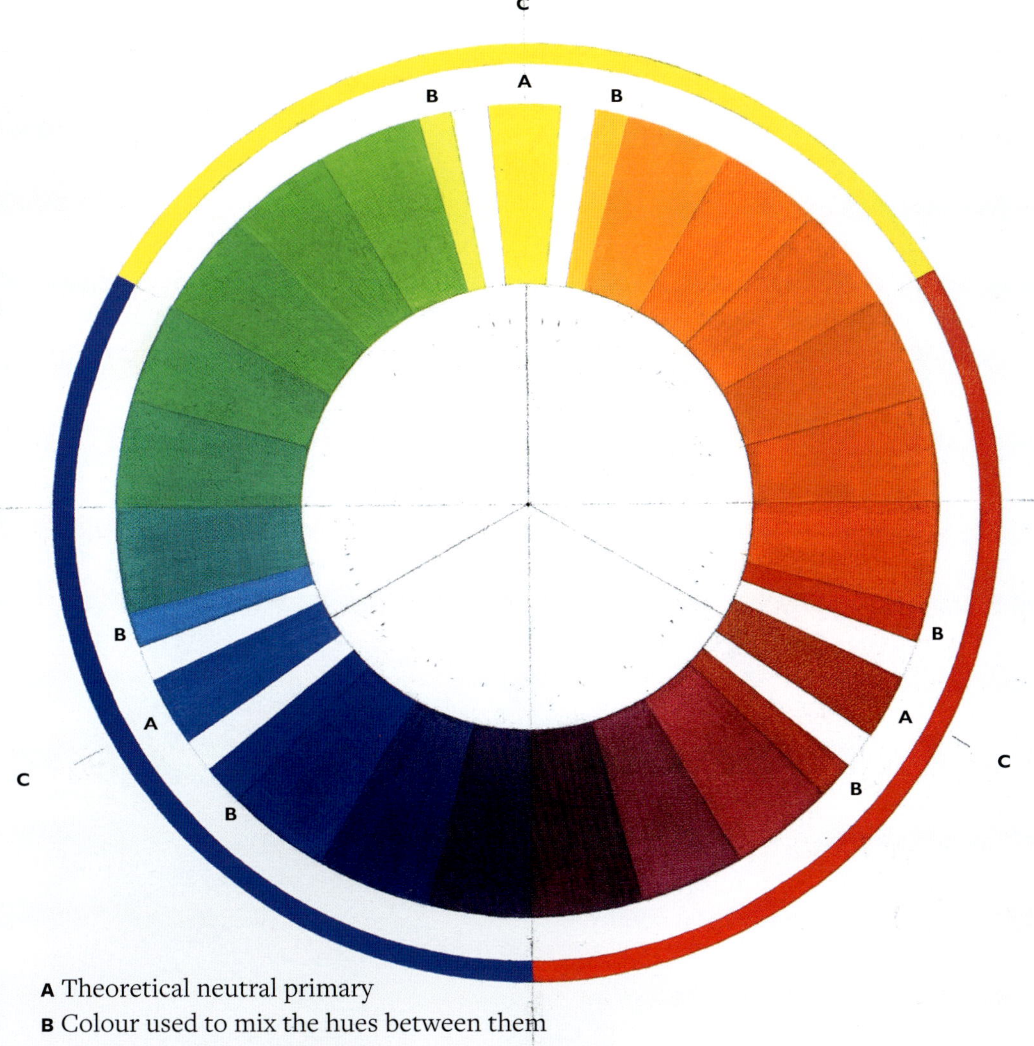

A Theoretical neutral primary
B Colour used to mix the hues between them
C Dominant primary influence

As I said at the beginning of this section, the concept of temperature in colour is purely perceptual. What isn't perceptual is the way this formula provides a practical and visual way to explain certain interactions of colour using temperature as a point of reference. The concept of this primary colour bias over spectrum colours will, I hope, really help artists understand how their colours interact. Whether using temperature as a basis is helpful or not will remain to be seen, but it helps me, so may I recommend it to you as well.

Similarly, we can use the concept of temperature to help us to match secondary and primary colours to one another. As we've seen in the section on Value (see page 36), when a primary colour is added to its matched complementary colour, it will produce some level of desaturation until eventually complete colour neutrality is achieved, resulting in either black or grey. Temperature, however, is key in this process as well, as the complementary colour needed to neutralise a primary, and vice versa, happens to usually be its temperature opposite. For example, a warm red will need a cool green complementary match. Coincidentally, temperature provides us with a clear way to visualise this, and it is certainly much easier to remember warm-to-cool and vice versa, than trying to table the respective quantities of each primary colour influence in the process.

Finally, it is worth dwelling on how deeply this feeling of warmth, or coolness, in connection to colour is rooted within our psyche and pervades our perception of temperature. Colour isn't just a scientific phenomenon to be measured and studied, it is part of the fabric of our reality. We see colour and, instantly, an emotion or sensation can be evoked in the viewer. A huge range of emotional and psychological stimuli are attached to seeing colour. To separate our emotional experience of colour from the study of it is like listening to music only to count the notes and observe the structure without letting it do what it was created to do: move the soul.

It's also curious that while adding the warm hemisphere of hues to the cool will generally only desaturate and/ or darken those colours, adding the blue hemisphere of hues to the reds not only desaturates them, but the blues actually seem to rob the warm colours of their life and vibrancy too.

These effects may be purely psychosomatic, but it's curious nonetheless that vibrancy, life and daylight are inextricably linked in our subconscious with the warm yellow, orange and red range of colours, and the blue range of colours are the antithesis of these, representing the extinguishing of heat, life, colour and the coming of night, where, if there is light, it's generally blue, the destroyer of saturation (cue dramatic music).

Transparency *and* Opacity

A much overlooked aspect of colour in paint is transparency and opacity. This can be a confusing and, at times, frustrating aspect, but it is essential to tackle if you are to really master the use of colour in your work.

The confusion starts from the word 'go', as most tubes of paint have a transparency and opacity rating on them. This purports to be helpful, but there are transparent colours that are transparent when painted thinly yet semi-opaque when applied thickly. And then there are 'semi-transparent' colours. Are they transparent? Slightly transparent? A little less opaque than a similar hue? It's an artist's nightmare.

Let me try to shed a little light. Broadly speaking, most paint colours fall into either the transparent or opaque categories. 'Semi-transparent' isn't particularly helpful. Within these categories, any colour can usually be adapted to make it transparent, as we will see.

Dark pure colours, such as magenta (PR122), ultramarine blue (PB29), phthalocyanine blue (PB15) and phthalocyanine green (PG7), are transparent. In fact, most primary and secondary colours are mostly transparent. The exceptions to this rule are the cadmium colours: cadmium red, orange, yellow and green, for example. All cadmiums are beautifully opaque. Pyrrole red (PR254) is also opaque.

That only really leaves black, white and tertiary colours such as the umbers: raw umber, burnt umber (both PBr7, which is confusing – one is cooked and one isn't, but you'd think they'd differentiate with the number!) and other oxides such as Venetian red and burnt sienna (both PBr7 again – it's a pigment of many uses – but they are also sometimes made with PR101 synthetic iron oxide instead). These colours are reasonably opaque, or at least cover well, and it's this ability to cover what is beneath the paint that generally makes a pigment opaque or appear to be opaque.

Lastly, there are black and white. Most blacks are fantastic at covering what they're painted over. Their ability to desaturate and destroy saturation (chroma) gives the impression at least of opacity and this is the case with most of the dark colours. Ultramarine blue (PB29), for instance, is transparent when painted very thinly, but it's also so dark that it can sometimes seem opaque, as it's difficult to see through when painted on thickly, plus it's naturally reasonably dark.

The most popular white is titanium white (PW6), which truly is opaque. Zinc white (PW4) is more transparent and mixes well with other colours, although recent studies suggesting that this pigment can be brittle and lead to cracking have made it unpopular with most artists. Lead white (PW1) is like zinc white (PW4) in opacity and far superior in many ways, but it's also banned in most countries, so is appropriately difficult to find and use.

THE SCIENCE OF TRANSPARENCY AND OPACITY

How opaque or transparent a paint is depends entirely on how light is reflected back at the viewer. If a paint is opaque, light is reflected straight back off the layer of pigment, with none being reflected from the surface below the pigment layer. When a paint has any transparency, some light will pass through the pigment layer and illuminate both the surface below the paint and also the pigment surface, meaning both layers can be seen.

You can see opposite that under a microscope the white looks dull and not very white at all. This is because titanium white is opaque, and light is reflected largely from its surface when we use it as paint. However, magenta (PR122) is transparent and is illuminated in the slide like a stained-glass window, with the light from the microscope's mirror being able to shine through the particles and light up the colour from underneath. If you painted magenta (PR122) on a white surface, you would get much the same effect, with light being able to pass through the transparent film of colour and reflect from the surface of the canvas or panel illuminating the colour.

The Attributes *of* Colour

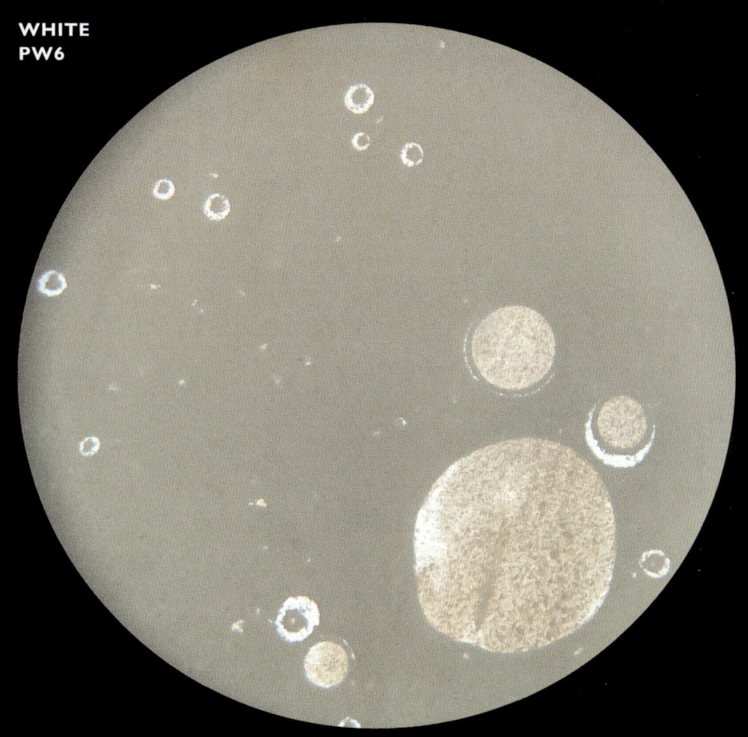

WHITE
PW6

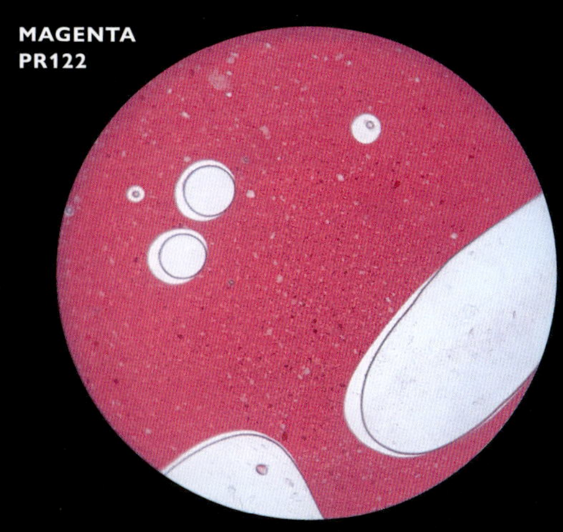

MAGENTA
PR122

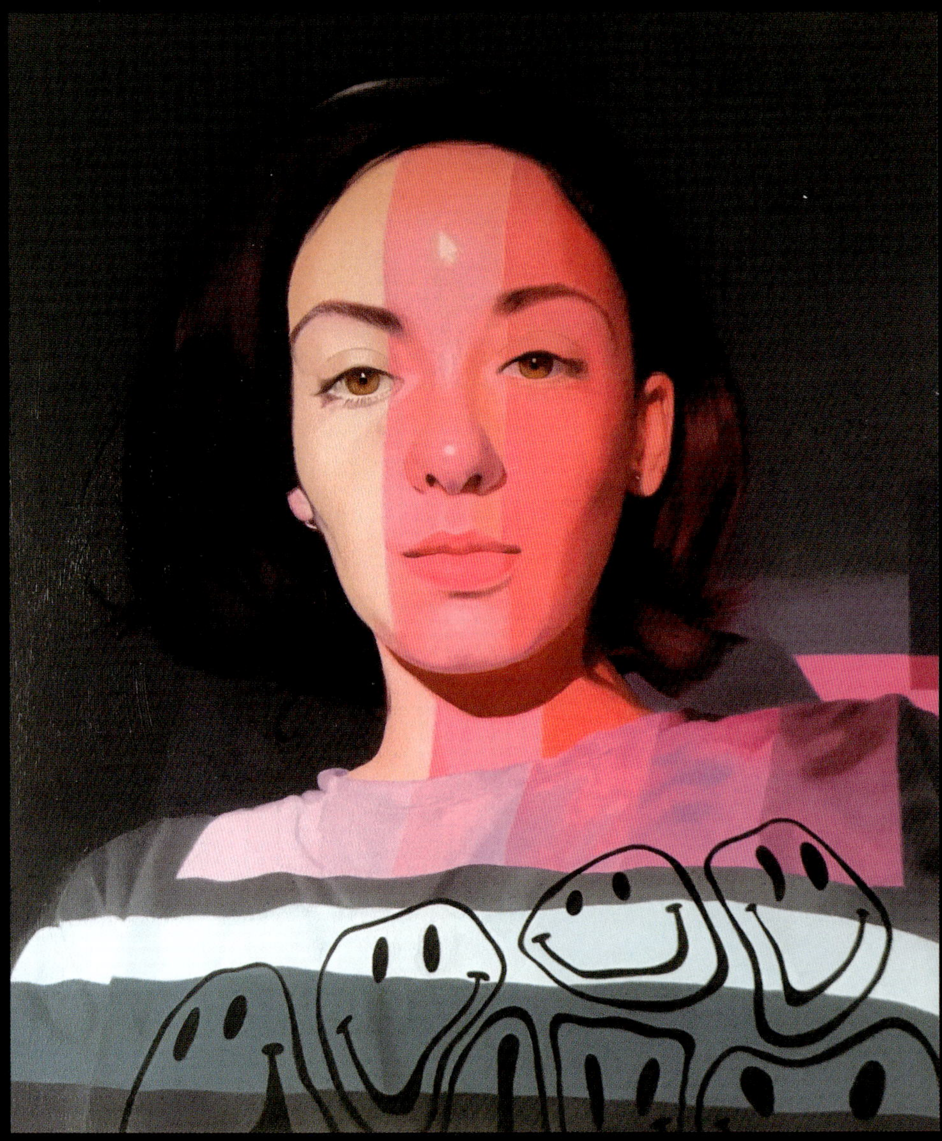

INCREASING OPACITY OR TRANSPARENCY

Any paint colour can be made more transparent by the addition of a diluent (any substance that dilutes another). With oil paint, it's usually oil or solvent that's used; with watercolour, it's water, and the same with acrylic paint. There are also innumerable 'glaze mediums' used by artists, but the most basic medium is oil: linseed, safflower or walnut. Whatever magical concoction you find, or come up with, the principle is the same: you are diluting the paint by adding a medium that will disperse the pigment particles to enable you to see through them.

Sometimes, I use a thinned titanium white (PW6) with linseed oil to create a glaze and paint this over the background to give the illusion of bringing the subject forward by diminishing the colours around it with the white glaze. In the picture opposite, however, I used a glaze to increase saturation. With this painting, I was aiming for as much saturation as possible and the only way to do this was to add more pure colour.

By way of a brief description, my glazing technique for paintings such as this is as follows. I take a paint colour and add oil (or glaze medium) to the colour until it makes a very fluid mixture, the consistency of single cream. I paint this on roughly until the area I'm glazing over is covered. I then brush it out and smooth it with a very clean and dry synthetic, flat wash-type brush, wiping off the excess paint on the brush with a clean cloth to keep the brush clean, until the colour that's left is almost more like a stain than a film of paint.

You do need to ensure that what you are painting over is completely dry, and avoid using any thinners if you can, or use them very carefully, as they can reactivate or remove the dried paint underneath. The more you work the glaze, the greater the chance you could damage the layer underneath, so it is worth practising this technique before trying it out on a painting that matters.

Left *Juana*, painted utilising glazes of Magenta (PR122 and PV19) and Phthalocyanine Green (PG7) to enhance the saturation/chroma of the underlying colours.

Glazing can also be used to change colours, optically mixing them on the painted surface. In the diagram opposite, I've painted warm and cool versions of each primary colour in three-square strips. The single-colour square on the right (A) is the colour that has been used as a glaze over the two on the left (B). The two half-squares underneath the two on the left (C) show the colour that has been glazed over.

You can see that overall, the darker colours work better as glazes than the lighter colours, and that the value of the colour being painted over also influences the outcomes of the resultant mixes. These secondary colours are being created by the layers mixing optically, rather than the more typical process where we would premix the colours together on the palette first before applying to the canvas.

Although I haven't explored this much in my own work, I imagine there are some very interesting applications for this technique of adapting colour on the painted surface in art. Glazing has sadly dropped out of popularity now, but in the past, it was used widely in fine art painting and to great effect. This is a technique worth investing time learning.

The Attributes *of Colour*

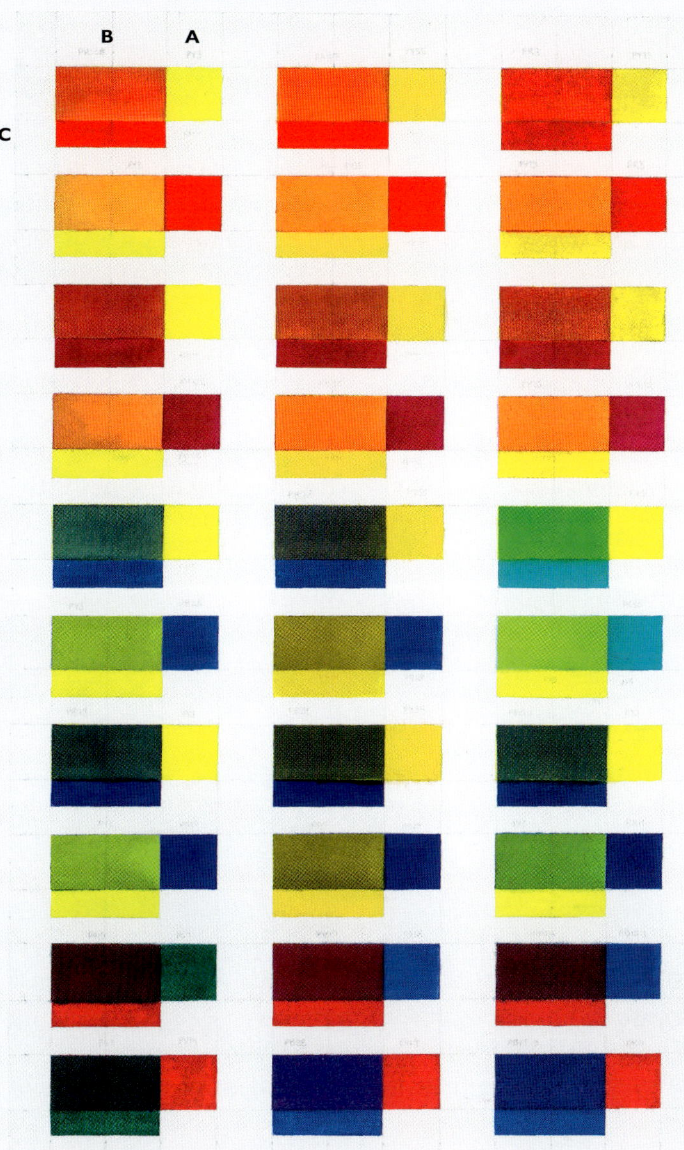
B
A
C

The opposite of transparency is, of course, opacity, and while it doesn't always yield the exciting results you can get from glazing, it is nonetheless a subject worth looking into.

The issue I usually encounter is a lack of opacity in more transparent colours, many of which are intense and loaded with colour potential, but which are difficult to apply as paint. This is where we can borrow opacity from other colours. The usual route for this is to reach for titanium white (PW6), but you may have noticed that titanium white tends to deaden the vibrancy of many colours if used in excess.

The key to knowing how much white to add is found in the value of the colour you wish to modify. If it's a very dark colour, you can apply the Goldilocks principle to retain saturation: introduce just enough white to bring your colour out of the gloom, but not so much that you wash it out.

White works wonderfully well to add opacity in colours such as magenta (PR122) and the dark, transparent phthalocyanine blues and greens. If you add white carefully to these colours, they will yield a vibrant and vivid range of hues. In fact, there is a whole range

of usually expensive colours that can be produced easily and simply by just adding white to a cheaper pigment. Colours such as cerulean or cyan blue are often a mix of phthalocyanine blue (PB15) and titanium white (PW6); king's blue is a mix of ultramarine blue (PB29) and titanium white (PW6); a range of vivid pinks are often a mix of magenta (PR122) or permanent rose (PV19) with titanium white (PW6). Experimentation can demonstrate that the judicial use of a little opacity borrowed from titanium white (PW6) can save you a lot of money in creating your own colours.

Opacity can, of course, also be borrowed from sources other than white. The cadmium range of colours are great at lending their natural opacity to transparent hues without reducing saturation. For instance, cadmium lemon yellow (PY35) could be added to phthalocyanine blue (PB15) to create a vivid range of greens that would be much opaquer and easier to use than if you had added arylide/hansa lemon yellow (PY3), which like phthalocyanine blue (PB15) is transparent.

So, opacity can sometimes be borrowed from one colour and leant

    The Attributes of Colour

to another, and vice versa, depending on the application. Sometimes you might want a more transparent mix, sometimes a more opaque mix, but knowing which colours have that transparency or opacity can really help when producing the desired results.

Many of us struggle to handle transparent colours, as they slip about on the surface a bit when you apply them and take a lot more control in the brushwork to get good results, so adding a little opacity to the mix can really help in these situations. Just be careful of excess white use and be aware that cadmium colours are not only expensive, but they also need careful handling and disposal. However, if used responsibly, the opacity that comes from cadmium colours is incredibly helpful to the artist, even if they do take forever to dry.

Pure transparent colours may be the most difficult set of colours to master in terms of application, and most of the spectrum colours we have as paints fall into this category, but it really is worth taking the time to master this. My top tip is to use a fine synthetic brush if you want an even stroke. I mostly outlined the diagrams in this book with a small, round synthetic brush and then brushed the colour out smoothly with a flat synthetic brush that had enough paint in it to hold all the brush hairs together, so the brush was more like a smooth but hairy spatula, or spreader, than a brush where you could see the brush marks. Thankfully, you're more likely to use transparent colours in mixes, in this case in combination with an opaquer additional colour, which makes them far easier to use and apply.

2

The Primaries

Colour is an emotive subject. Armies are identified by the colours of the flags they fly while sports teams are proudly denoted by the colours of their strips. Even in colour theory, there is partisanship, with one camp fiercely defending its position against another. But imagine if we could combine the best bits of these theories and discard the rest.

In this section, we'll be looking at a key element of any colour theory: the primary colour sets. These are the colours that can be combined to create all the other colours on the spectrum. They are normally found in groups of threes, and it can be a surprise to discover that there are more options than the red-yellow-blue combination we learn in primary school. A solid understanding of the primary colours, and the different primary colour sets, is essential for any artist working with pigment. Let's look at the options.

RGB: Red – Green – Blue

First up is the primary colour set favoured by lighting technicians and digital artists: RGB, or red, green and blue (see the diagram opposite). This is an additive colour set and is largely relevant when looking at colour in light, particularly modern screen technology. Thanks to early pioneers such as James Clerk Maxwell (1831–79), Thomas Young (1773–1829) and Hermann von Helmholtz (1821–94), the RGB colour set has given us valuable insights into how we perceive the world around us. However, as we shall see, this colour set doesn't work when applied in paint.

In the top diagram opposite, I mocked up in paint what appears in light when red, green and blue are combined. In the bottom diagram, I show what actually happens if I combine these colours in paint. By comparing these two diagrams we can see that although RGB colours mix beautifully in light (or non-physical colour), they don't mix very well at all in paint (physical colour). When it comes to mixing paint, it is best to disregard this set of primaries.

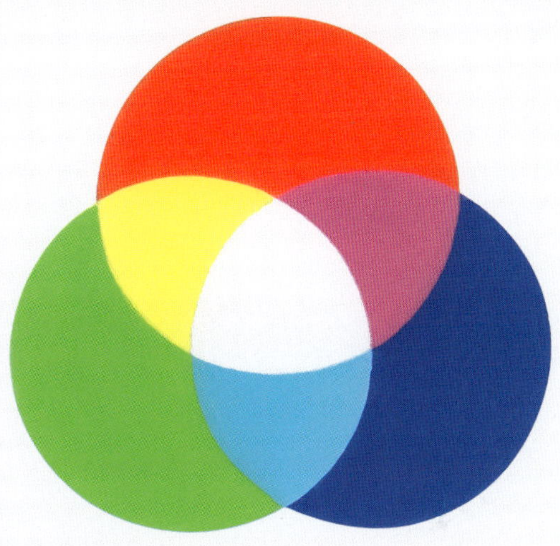

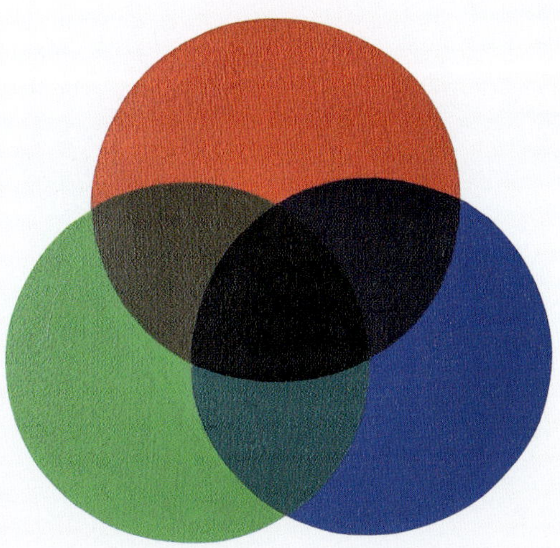

Above The RGB colour set mocked up to show how it appears in light
Below The RGB colour set as it actually appears in paint

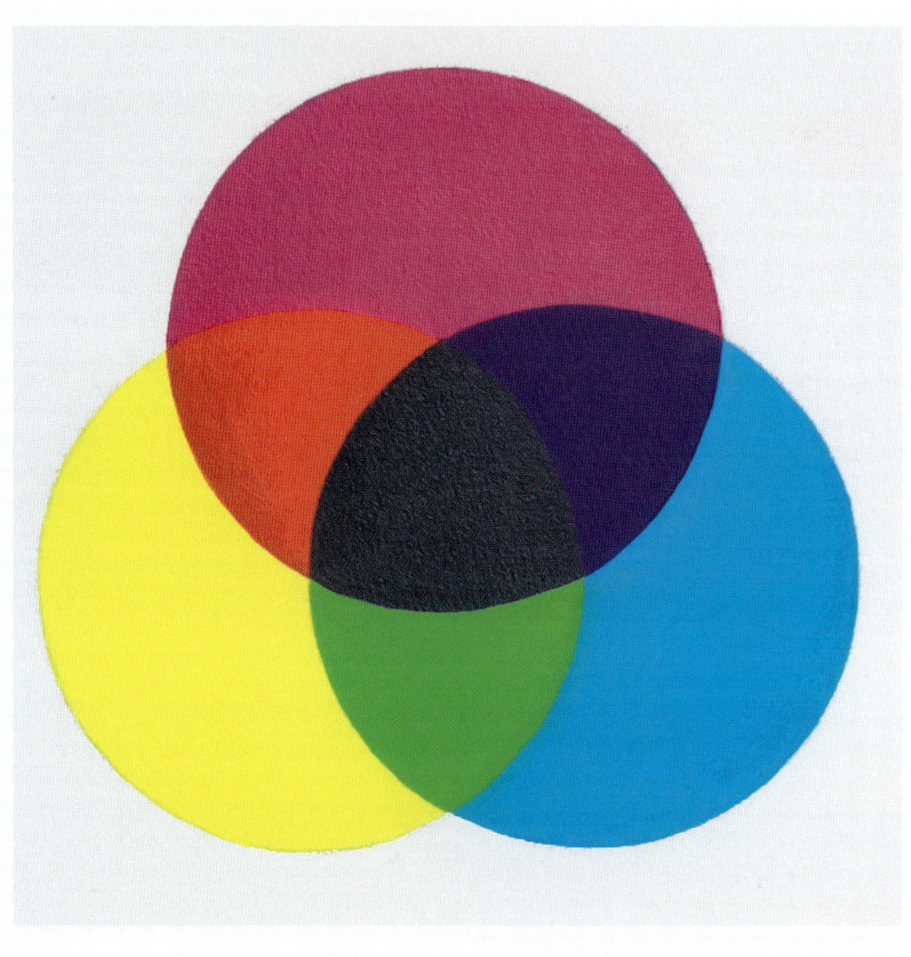

CMY: Cyan – Magenta – Yellow

Next up is CMY, or cyan, magenta and yellow. This set was developed for the four-colour printing process used in printed material (such as this book). The fourth colour refers to K for key or keyline (and not, as is sometimes thought, kohl).

The black, or key, colour is added in the printing process because C + M + Y can make, or give the illusion of, a great range of colours and greys by laying them beside or on top of one another in thin films of printing ink, but not always a very reliable black.

The dots in four-colour process lay beside one another to give the visual illusion of other colours, and they occasionally overlap. So, while the CMY set of primaries works very well in print, it does have its weakness as a primary colour set for use in paint.

As you can see in the painted CMY model opposite, it can make excellent greens and adequate-to-good purples, but very poor oranges, which end up a little muted and brown. This is because magenta is a very cool red and not adjacent to orange on the spectrum; it contains too much of a blue bias.

Choosing the correct shades of CMY in paint is also quite a subjective challenge. Our main source for magenta in paint is quinacridone magenta (PR122), which is quite dark, transparent and very cool with a blue bias. To make it look more like 'process magenta' (the magenta used in four-colour printing) in the diagram, I've had to add a little white to the magenta to lighten it, which isn't ideal. The other alternative is quinacridone red/rose (PV19), which is good but a little too warm. The cyan is also rather subjective. The closest colour I've found as a paint is cobalt teal (PG50), and I've had to add cobalt blue (PB28) to this to make it bluer. A tint of a phthalocyanine blue (PB15) made by adding white works too. Finally, in paint you have a cool lemon yellow (PY3 or similar) or a warm yellow such as cadmium yellow (PY35). There isn't an entirely neutral yellow, but in practice, do we really need one?

RYB: Red – Yellow – Blue

Finally, we have the subtractive colour model standard, RYB, or red, yellow and blue. This is the one you likely learnt about at school, when you first encountered mixing colour in paint. As you can see from the results opposite, when this is mixed in paint, we achieve a better result than either of the paint-mixed RGB or CMY.

The orange is very good, the green is good, and the purple is good too. The problem that you immediately encounter with this set is that it's extremely difficult, if not impossible, to find those mythical unicorn colours – neutral versions of red, yellow and blue – needed to make it work. As we saw earlier, each colour has its own biases and temperature (see page 68), and that means a red will either lean towards blue or yellow, and rarely will it sit perfectly in the middle. Sometimes the biases in the primaries will match and work, but other times they will add unwanted colour via the biases, creating a poor mix.

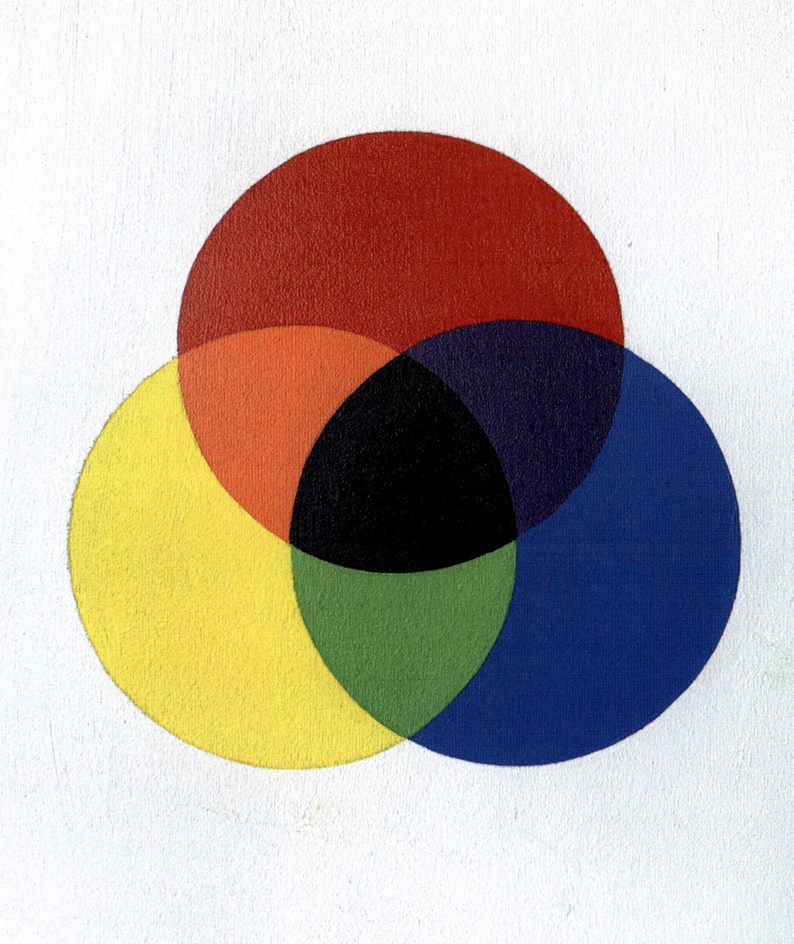

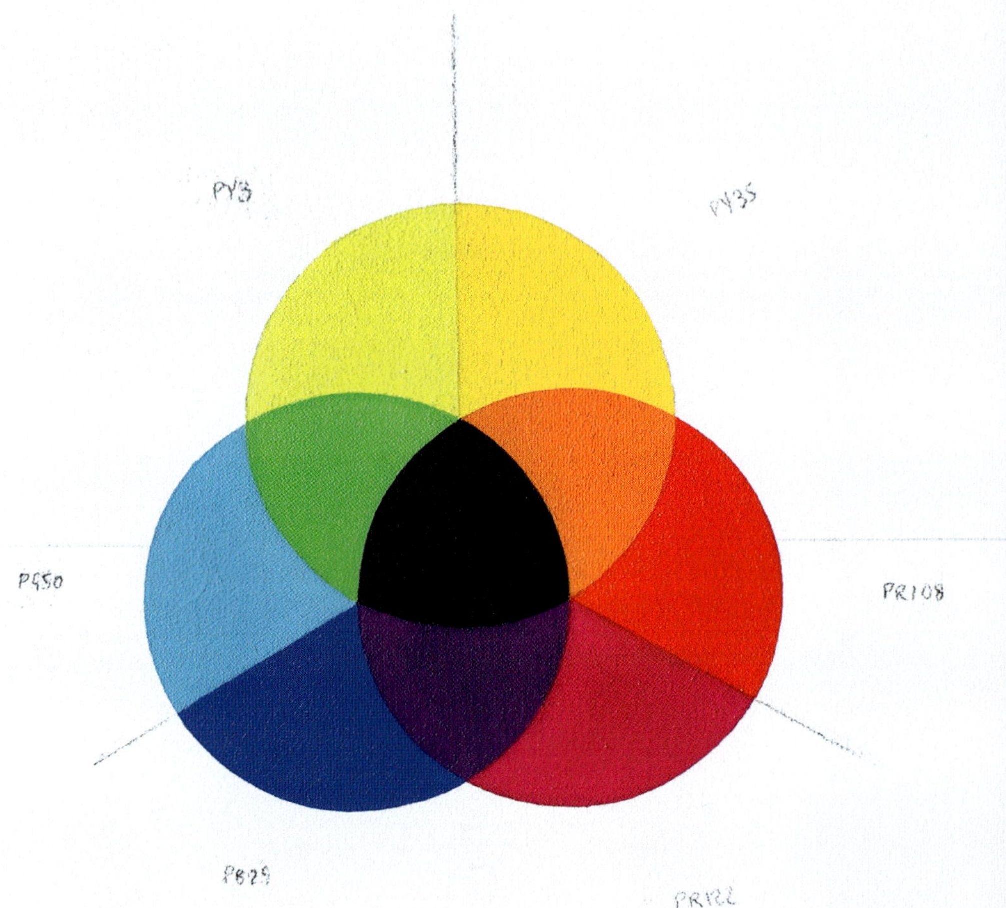
PY3
PY35
PG50
PR108
PB29
PR122

The Search *for the* Perfect Primaries

The question remains: why do we feel the need to use only one set of primaries? Each primary colour has a temperature bias based on its position on the spectrum, so why don't we work *with* this, instead of needlessly trying to work against it?

When it comes to colour theory, there are a surprising number of different camps, each defending one way of looking at colour as opposed to another, and far be it for me to suggest any dogmatic improvements to the classic 'three primary colour' sets. However, I have found that by taking the bits that work in one painted diagram and combining them with the bits that work in the others, I have created an alternative route that perhaps offers an improvement on an existing model.

Most of the primary colour sets we've seen have their strengths and weaknesses, so as suggested at the start of this chapter, why not discard the weaknesses and combine the strengths of each? May I humbly suggest an alternative, a kind of United Nations of primary colour sets if you will. In the final primaries diagram shown on the left, I've paired the primaries.

This is a kind of RYB/CMY hybrid, but I've placed the adjacent (more about this later) versions of each primary next to one another. So, cool yellow is next to its spectrum partner, cyan, and warm yellow is next to its neighbour, warm red, and magenta is next to warm blue, where it should be. They're still essentially RYB but enhanced (red = warm red and cool magenta, yellow = warm and cool yellows, blue = cool cyan and warm blue).

By using pairs of each primary, you can achieve excellent versions of each secondary colour. You can see from the diagram on page 97 what happens if you reverse these primary pairs.

In the diagram opposite, I've
switched the pairs so the primaries
furthest away from one another on
the spectrum are next to one another
in the Venn diagram. As you can see,
 a doubling of the blue bias in both the
lemon yellow and the magenta make
a very brown orange, the doubling of
the red bias in the warm yellow and
warm blue make a very olive green, and
the warm red and cyan make an almost
colour-neutral desaturated purple, as
there are strong yellow overtones in
both the cyan and the warm red, and all
three primaries when mixed together
will incline towards colour neutrality.

With the wheel, we are still working
with only three primary colours, but
we are using a pair of each, one visually
warm and one visually cool. If we
match these, the colour theory works
well and achieves excellent results for
all our secondary colours.

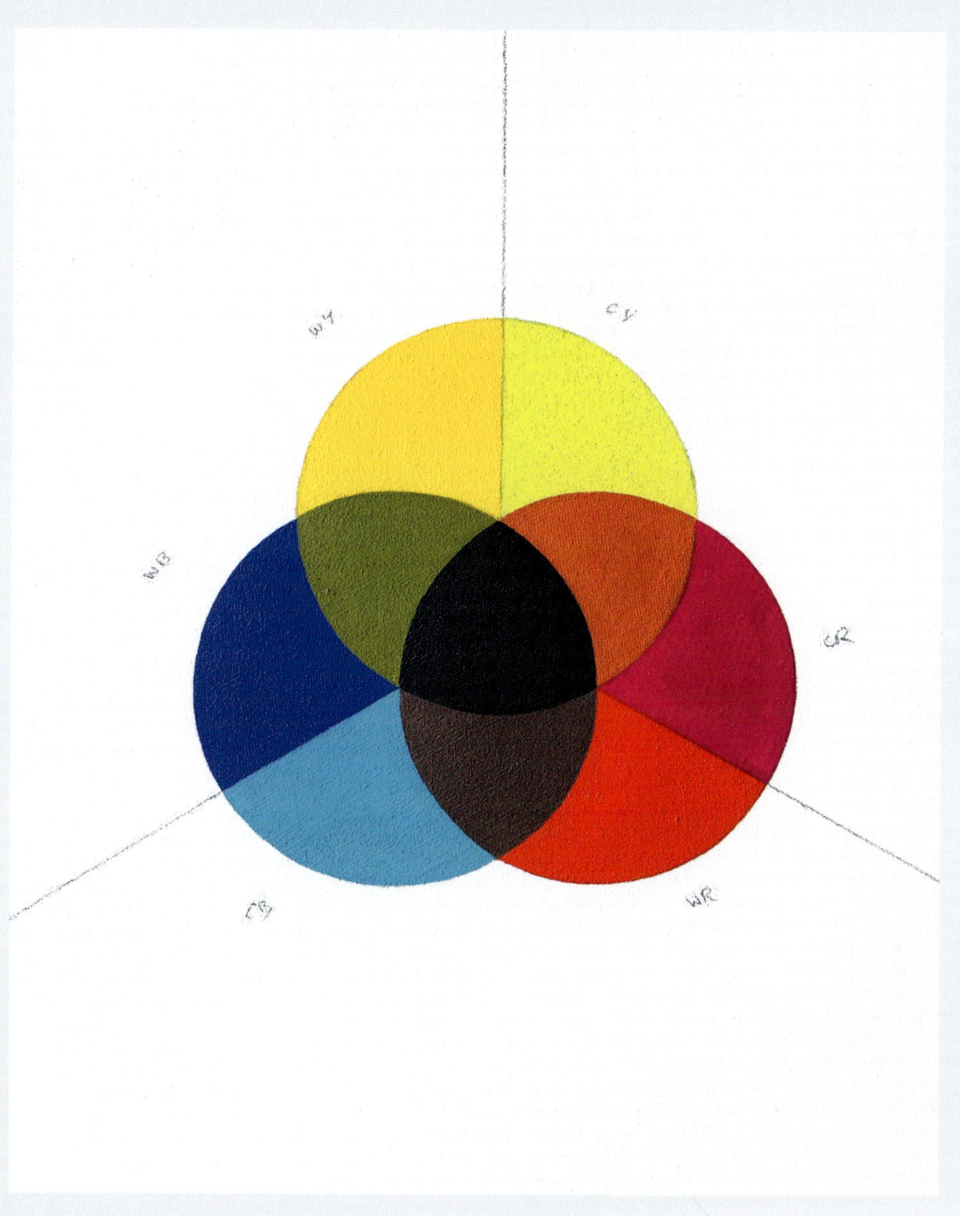
WY
CY
WB
CR
CB
WR

3

Colour Mixing

Colour Adjacency *and* Bias:
A recap

When it comes to colour mixing, the most important things to be aware of are the biases of your initial colours. As we saw in the attributes of colour in Chapter 1, there are very few, if any, 'pure' colours in paint; every colour we use comes with a bonus free colour thrown in. A red, for instance, will be easily recognised and named as red, but perhaps trickier to identify will be its bias. With red, the bias will be either yellow or blue, a yellow bias making it a warm red and a blue bias making it a cool red.

If we look at the diagram above right, I've painted two of each primary colour in terms of visual temperature (one on either side of neutral) and two of each secondary colour to try and keep things simple.

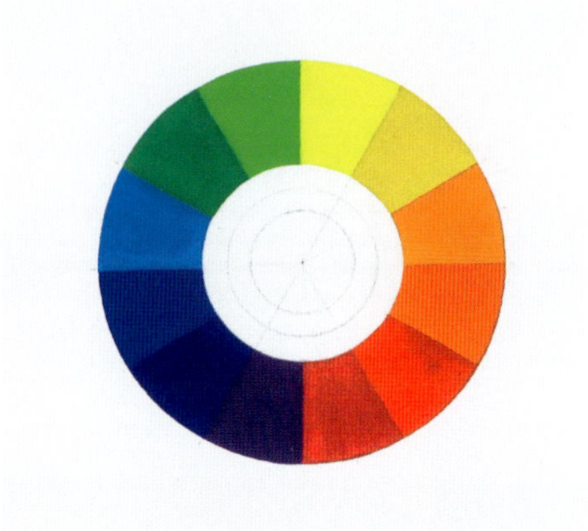

In the diagram opposite, I've added partial rings in primary colours around the outside to show the extent of the inclusion, or influence, of those primary colours on the other hues. Blue (A) is present in all the hues from cool yellow to cool red, as all of the hues from cool yellow through green, blue (of course), purple and cool red all contain the influence of blue in them. Red (B) is present in warm yellow through all the hues to warm blue, and yellow (C) can be found from cool blue all the way round to warm red. Each primary colour has an equal influence over all the others.

Colour Mixing

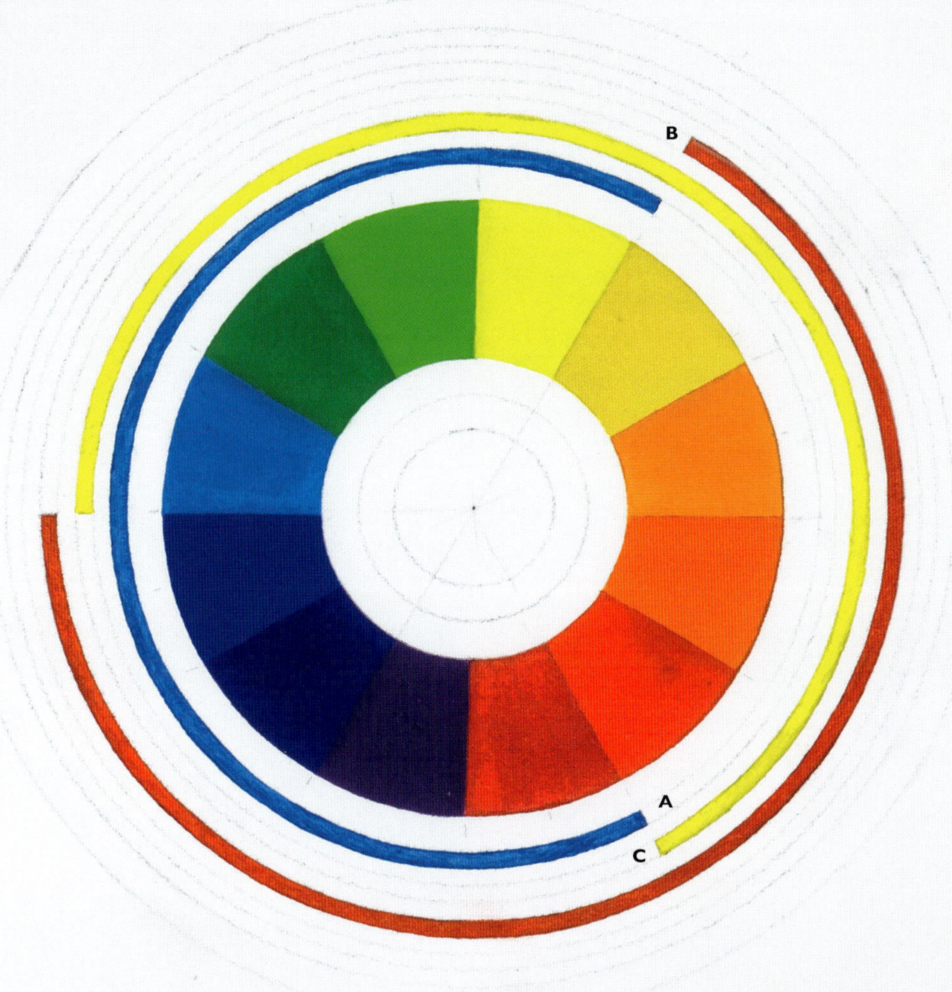
B
A
C

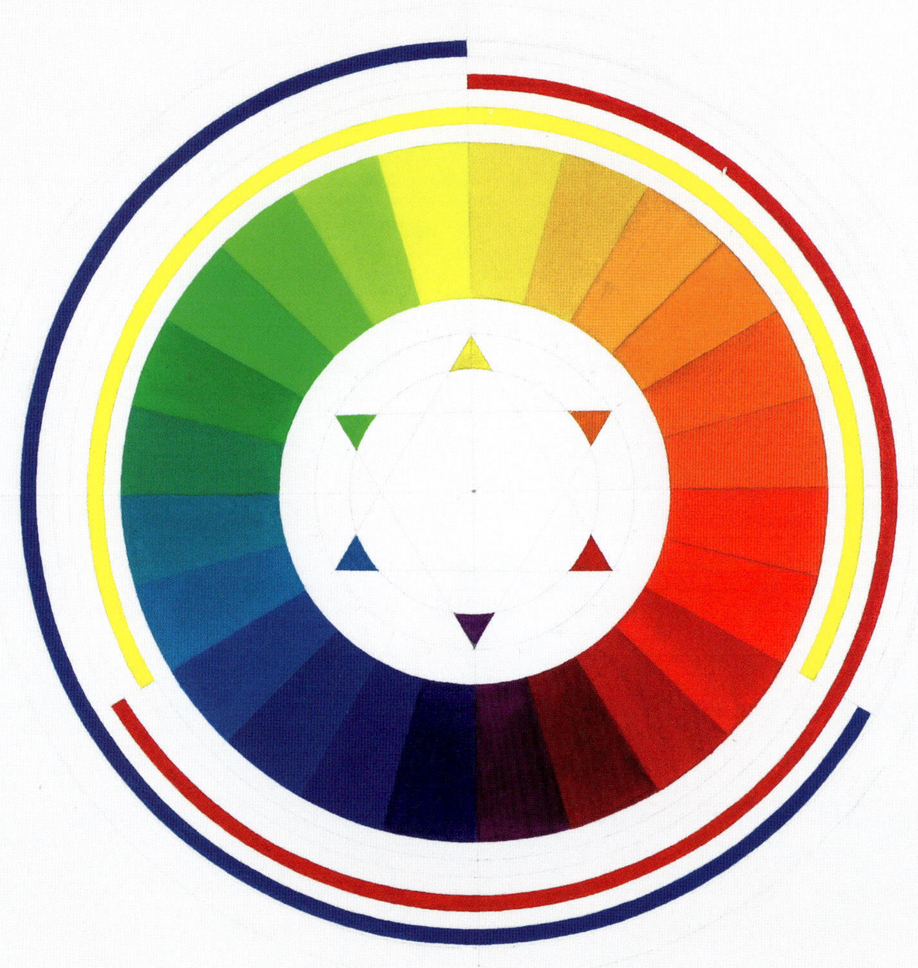

In the diagram on the left, I've expanded the amount of hues. The triangular pointers indicate a theoretical neutral point in each of the primary and secondary colours, and the outer rings serve the same purpose as those of the second diagram (page 101), indicating the influence or bias of the primary colours in all of the rest. Basically, each colour on the colour wheel encompassed by an outer primary colour ring will contain traces of that primary colour within it.

If you look at the cool yellow to the left of the central neutral primary and go to the end of the green section, you will eventually come to the cool blue version of the blue primary.

Now, blue and yellow make green, right? So, you will ideally only want primaries that have only those colours in them to make pure greens. The cool blue has a yellow bias and the cool yellow has a blue bias, so they will match. If, however, you used a warm yellow or warm blue, you would be adding red to this mix, as warm blue and warm yellow, in a way, both contain traces of red and this would diminish the vibrancy of the mixes and turn them a little brown. Matching the bias as well as the primary colours will result in much cleaner, more vibrant hues.

Thankfully, the spectrum is a great guide to getting these mixes right. Either side of the neutral primaries on the spectrum are their warm and cool versions. By pairing cool blue to cool yellow, you will make the full range of vibrant greens in between. Likewise, by pairing warm yellow to warm red you will be able to mix the full range of oranges. Finally, by pairing and mixing warm blue with cool red you can create the full range of purples. This is because you are only mixing primaries that match in terms of primary colour and bias; they are *adjacent* to one another on the colour circle.

So, to mix orange, for instance, you would pick the warm yellow adjacent to it on the colour wheel and the warm red adjacent to it on the other side. Picking colours adjacent to the target colour when mixing secondaries will always result in the best possible match, if your goal is to mix pure colours. In fact, this is a great method for finding many colours. If you have, or can mix, the two colours either side of the target colour, then combining these two will usually yield the colour you're after – the one in the middle. I use this method all the time to find skin tones for portraits.

We can see perhaps the clearest demonstration of matching biases in the diagrams that appear opposite, which either match or mismatch the primaries.

If only one primary is mismatched – for instance, you have a warm yellow and a cool blue – the resultant green won't be as brown, but it will be less pure than matching cool yellow and cool blue. Where you have two mismatched biases, the bias is doubled and so its influence over the resultant mix is much greater.

Number 1 is warm yellow with its neighbour on the spectrum, orange. In real life, warm yellow is part of a continuum of hues that range from warm yellow to warm red and although the nearest neighbour to warm yellow is orange, the only difference between warm yellow and orange is the quantity of red; it's the red in the yellow that makes it orange. So, let's try to imagine that the extra colour (primary) in the warm yellow isn't orange, but red (2).

Let's take another example and look at cool yellow. This one is the other side of the mythical 'neutral' yellow and has a bias towards green on the spectrum, as it's closer to green than it is to orange. So, in this case (3), we can see a slice of green attached to the cool yellow because this is its neighbour on the spectrum. However, it's simpler to imagine that the extra hue in cool yellow is blue, so although you will see green in real life, try to imagine blue, as in number 4.

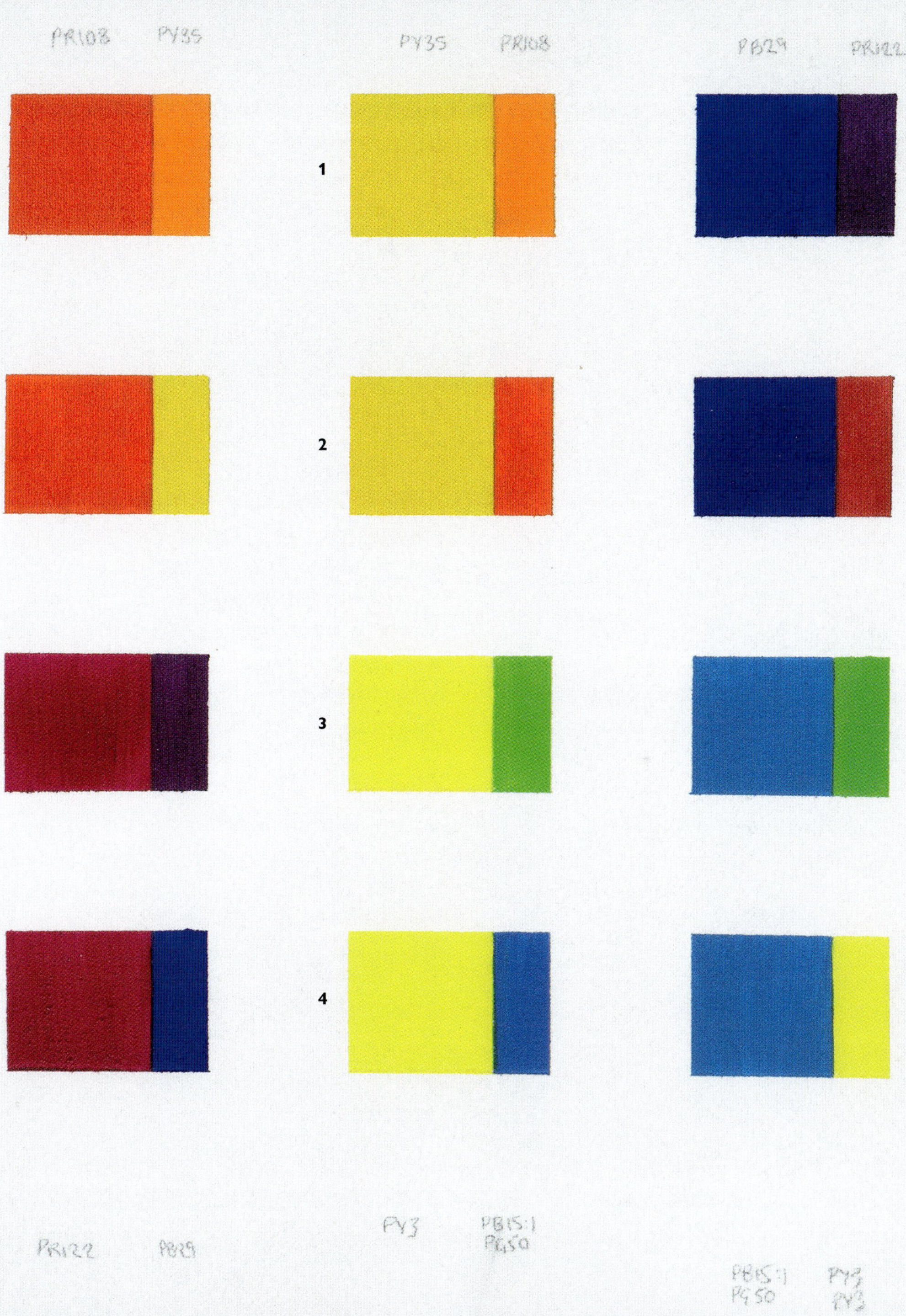

PR108   PY35
PY35   PR108
PB29   PR122
1
2
3
4
PR122   PB29
PR108   PY35
PY3   PB15:1
PG50
PB15:1   PY3
PG50   PR122

Colour mixing with colour biases in mind really boils down to colour maths. But don't worry if maths isn't your thing, it's really just a little simple arithmetic as follows:

1 (primary) + 1 (primary)
= 2 (secondary)

2 (secondary) + 1 (primary)
= 3 (tertiary)

1 (primary) + 1 (primary)
+ 1 (primary) = 3 (tertiary)

I expect that since you were very young, you've known that if you add one paint colour to another, you will make a new colour. For example, one splodge (technical term) of yellow and one splodge of blue will (usually) yield the colour green. The difficulty comes when you are trying to achieve a particular shade of the secondary colour, in which case you are likely to be disappointed unless you have picked up the basics of colour mixing.

Look at the two strips of red (1) and blue (2) opposite. You'll notice that from one end of the strip to the other, there is a wide variety of hues. Even this is only a limited sample of what's available. This is because many spectrum hues overlap, with one subtly merging into another. The cool blue (the one nearest the thin yellow bar) tends towards green, while the warm blue end (the one nearest the thin red bar) tends towards purple.

However, it's our primaries that mix to make our secondaries, so instead of a green bar at the cool end of the blue strip, I've put the primary closest to it on the spectrum – that is, yellow – and likewise for the others.

It follows that the red square closest to the yellow bar (the visibly warm red) is said to have a yellow bias, and the red on the other end has a blue bias. These biases are very important to take into account when mixing colours.

1

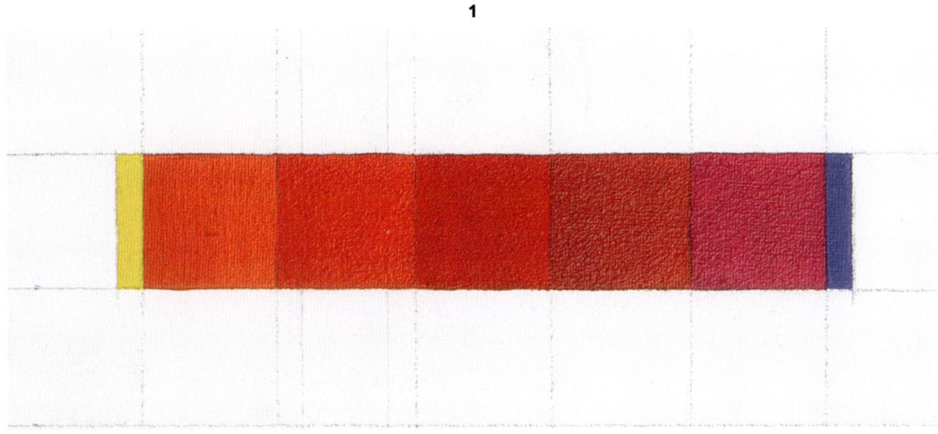

2

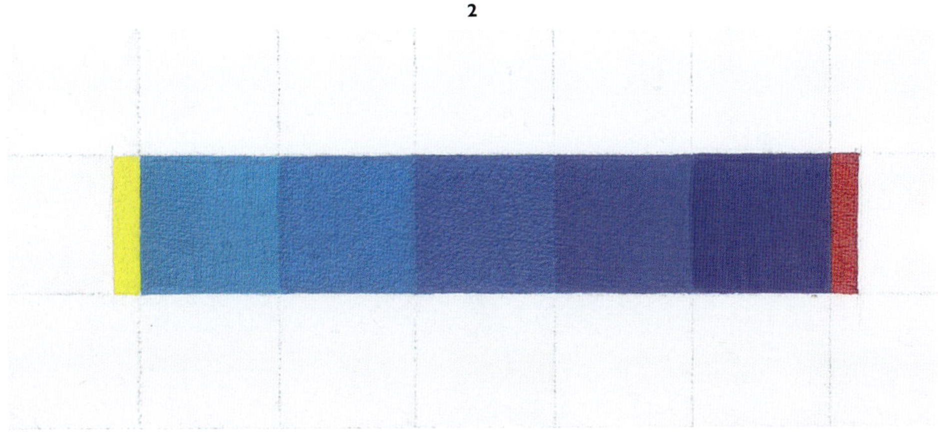

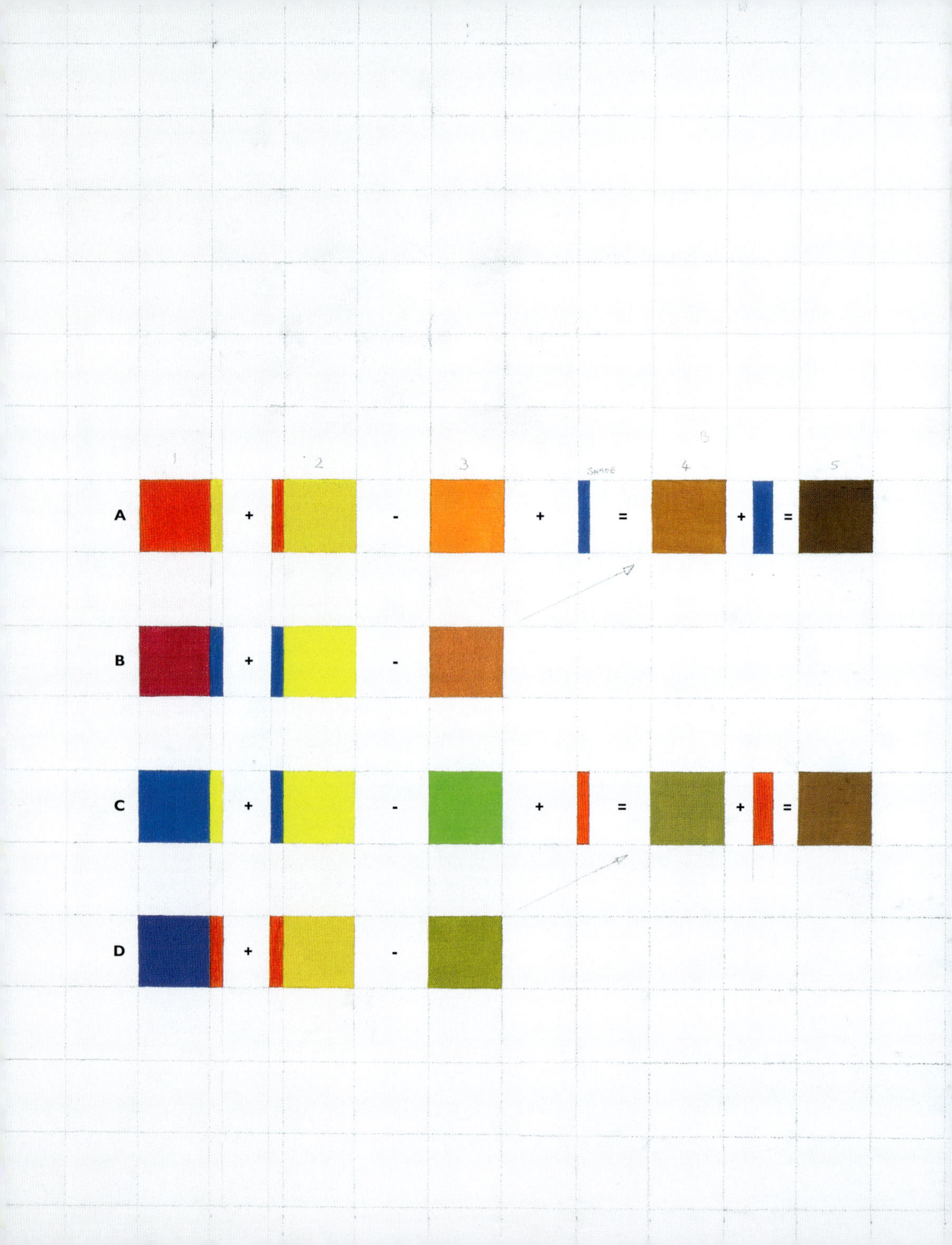

1   2   3   SHADE   4   5
A + - + = + =
B + -
C + - + = + =
D + -

Here are some more examples. If you look at the first red square, which is A1, I've added a thin yellow bar to indicate that this warm red has a yellow bias. Next to it, A2 is a warm yellow with a red bias, so it has a thin red bar. These biases match because they're adjacent to one another on the spectrum, so when they're combined to mix the orange in A3, the colour will be nice and clean.

In row B, however, when you combine B1 (magenta red) and B2 (lemon yellow), the result in B3 is a very brown orange. This is because both B1 and B2 have a strong blue bias, as indicated by the blue bars, and red + yellow + blue = brown. I've proved this by adding a little blue to A3, which results in A4, and A4 is very similar to the result in B3. Add more blue, as in A5, and the blue is doubled, making the resulting mix an even darker, less saturated brown.

If we repeat this experiment in row C and add C1 and C2 together, we get a clean, saturated green in C3, because the blue used has a yellow bias and yellow has a blue bias, so we're not adding the influence of any other primary colour.

In row D, however, I've picked a blue with a red bias and a yellow with a red bias, which when combined make D3, a rather murky green due to the added red influence from the two warm primaries. Again, I've added red to C3, resulting in C4, to prove that the addition of red will make a colour almost identical to the combination of D1 and D2. Add more red and this pushes the colour towards a warm orangey brown as in C5. Had the green in C3 been mixed using more blue, the result at C5 may well have been darker and more purple in nature.

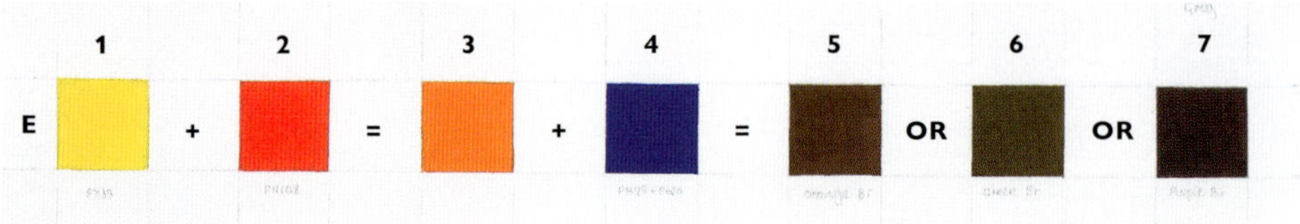

Let's take this further and look at some more examples. If you look at row E, I've used a yellow with a red bias (warm yellow) and red with a yellow bias (warm red). When you add a little blue with a red bias – in this instance, ultramarine blue (PB29) at E4 – the results can vary depending on the ratios of red and yellow used to make the orange, plus the ratio of the added blue here. You will either mix an orange-brown (E5) with a strong red + yellow bias, a green-brown (E6) with a strong blue + yellow bias or a purple-brown (E7) with a strong red + blue bias.

They're a little difficult to see, as the adding of a third primary colour via either the bias of your primaries or by physically adding a third primary colour paint will cause desaturation and muting of the mix. This adding of a third primary colour influence creates a tertiary colour. The good news is there are only four types of tertiary colours: they will either mix into an orange-brown, a green-brown, a purple-brown or, if you get the ratios just right, a neutral in the form of a grey or black.

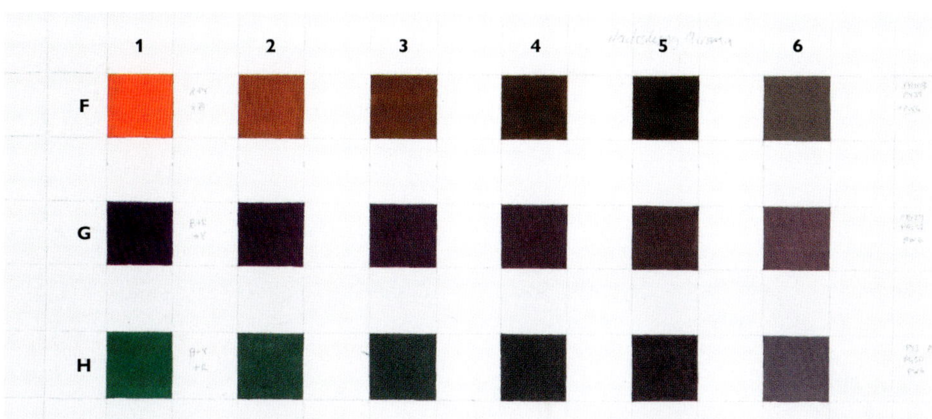

In the rows above, I've taken a secondary colour and added the missing of the three primaries to show how this desaturates the colour and can create grey or black. F1 is an orange (red + yellow) with a strong red bias. To this I've added blue incrementally to create the colours in F1–6. I've added a little white to the last square (F6) so you can see the neutrality a little better as a tint in a grey form.

Row G is a purple (red + blue) with a slight blue bias. To this I've incrementally added the missing primary again, in this case yellow, to show you how this diminishes the saturation and often darkens the mix. Again, the mix in G6 has had white added so you can see the grey that will result from adding white to G5.

Row H is green with a blue bias and has had red added to it, resulting in diminished saturation and darkening of the value.

In summary, it's very important to pair your colours correctly. To make pure secondaries, you will need adjacent primaries; primaries with matching colour biases. If you pick one or more secondary that brings to the mix the bias (influence) of another primary, other than those used to make your secondary, there will be a degree of desaturation and the colour will appear dull. This isn't so noticeable if only one primary is mismatched, but two mismatched primaries will double the influence of the bias and double the desaturation, muting your colour mix.

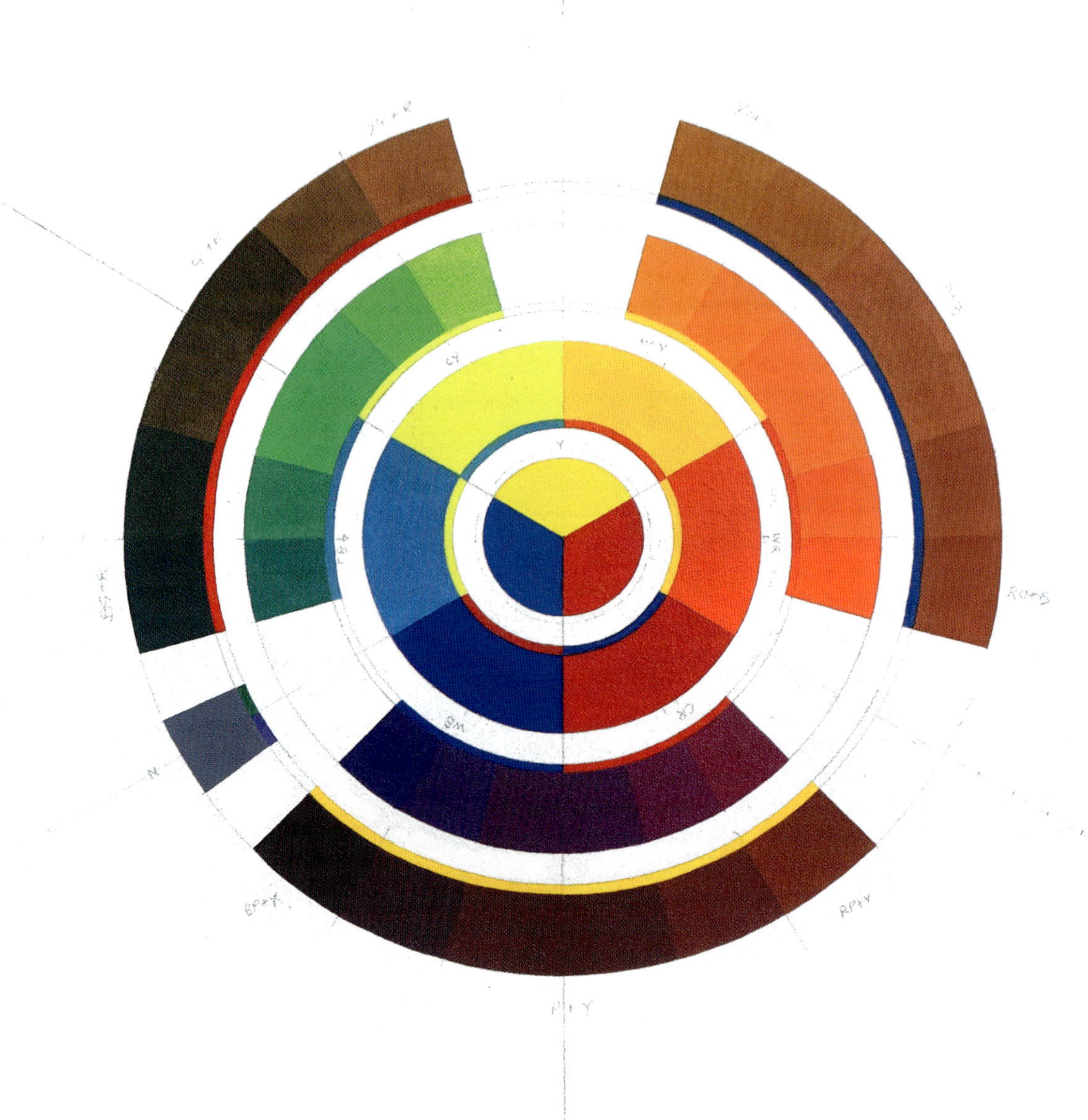

Colour Adjacency

In this diagram, I've started with the basics and worked outwards. The central section is divided into the three primaries (RYB). In the next ring, we have those three primaries split into their warm and cool versions. The thinner ring attached to this section shows the colour bias over each section. So, the cool yellow has a thin blue ring attached as it has a blue bias, warm yellow has a thin red ring attached as it has a red bias, and so on.

In the second ring, we have the secondary colours mixed from the colours in the primary colour ring. The thinner ring attached to this one shows the majority primary colour bias. So, looking at the orange section, the half above the yellow primary segment has a thin yellow ring indicating that this half of the orange hues has a dominant yellow bias, whereas the half above the red segment has a thin red ring showing that they have a red bias.

The third, outer, ring shows the tertiary colour mixes. These are the same colour as the second ring, but with the missing primary colours added. This is indicated by the thin ring. The orange section has had

blue added, the purple has had yellow added, and the green has had red added. Obviously, these mixes are dependent on the quantities of each colour used, but I've tried to get as accurate as I could.

You'll notice that each section still retains a strong influence from its secondary mix. The section above the oranges is still a warm orange-brown, the section above the purples has a strong purple/violet influence and the section above the greens is greenish. You can probably spot colours similar to the umbers here by the way.

You could swap out the cooler red for magenta and it would mix brighter purples if you wanted to recreate some of these mixes yourself. Also worth noting is that the purple section is very dark, so I've added a little white to make some of these more visible.

The purpose of this diagram is to show a kind of colour family tree, but I'm sure if you experiment with and adjust some of these colours, you could mix an even wider range yourself.

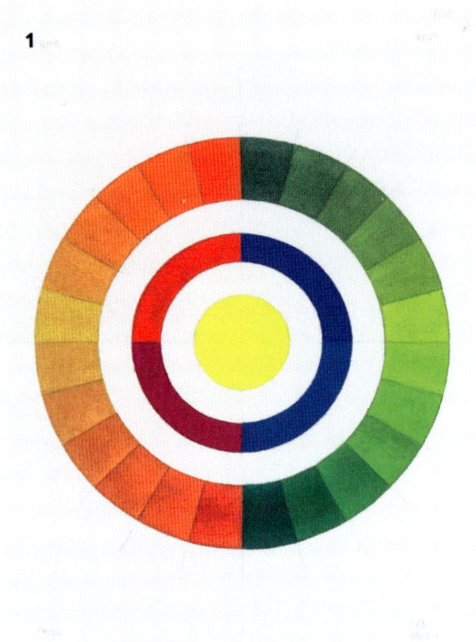

1

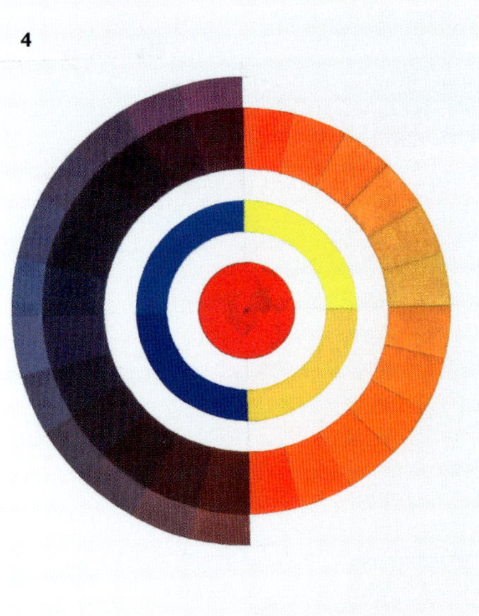

4

These next rings are variations on the bigger ring. The central circle is a primary colour of either a warm or cool temperature bias. The thinner ring is another primary colour split into warm and cool bias. The outer ring shows a range of results from mixing the central circle with the corresponding primary ring sections. Some of these have an extra partial ring added because the results were very dark, so again I mixed these with a little white to make the results more visible.

From each of these rings, those colours mixed using the adjacent colour mixing technique created the purest hues, as their biases matched, and no third primary colour influence was introduced. But where we have a doubling of non-matching biases, the colours are the most muted. For example, warm yellow and warm blue (having a red bias) mixed the brownest greens (3, top-right quadrant), but cool yellow and cool blue (having a blue or yellow bias) mixed the brightest greens (6, bottom-right quadrant), as they were free from the influence of a third primary.

Colour Mixing

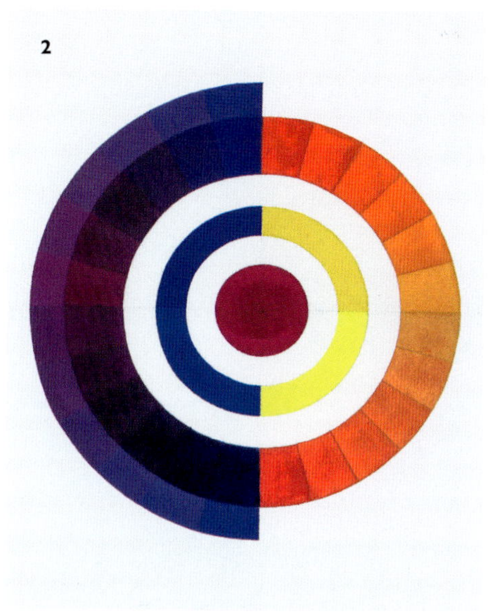

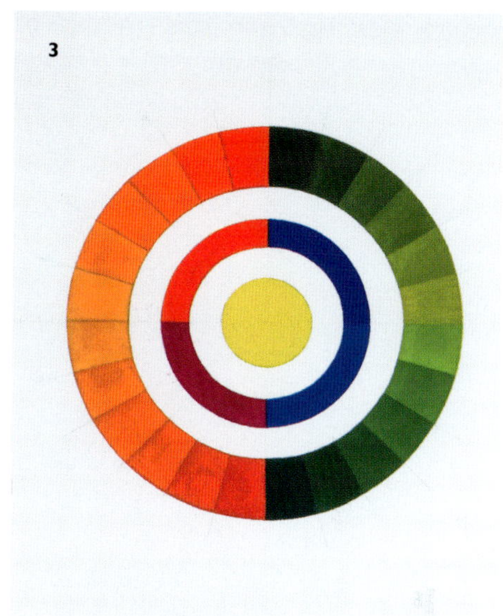

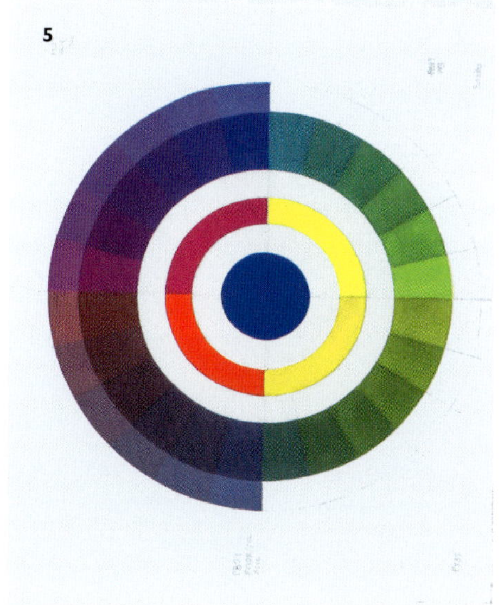

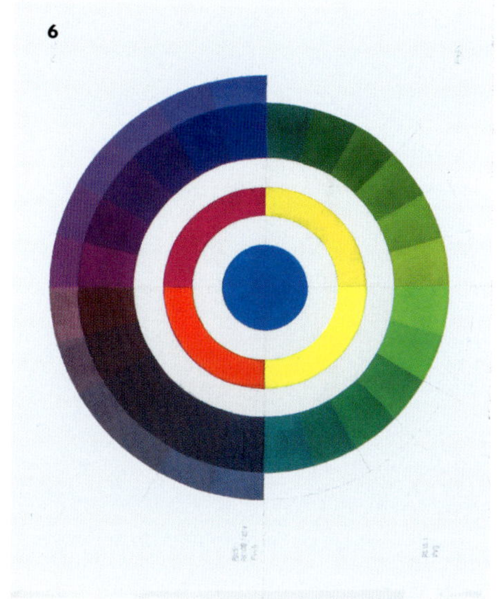

4

Interactions
of Colour

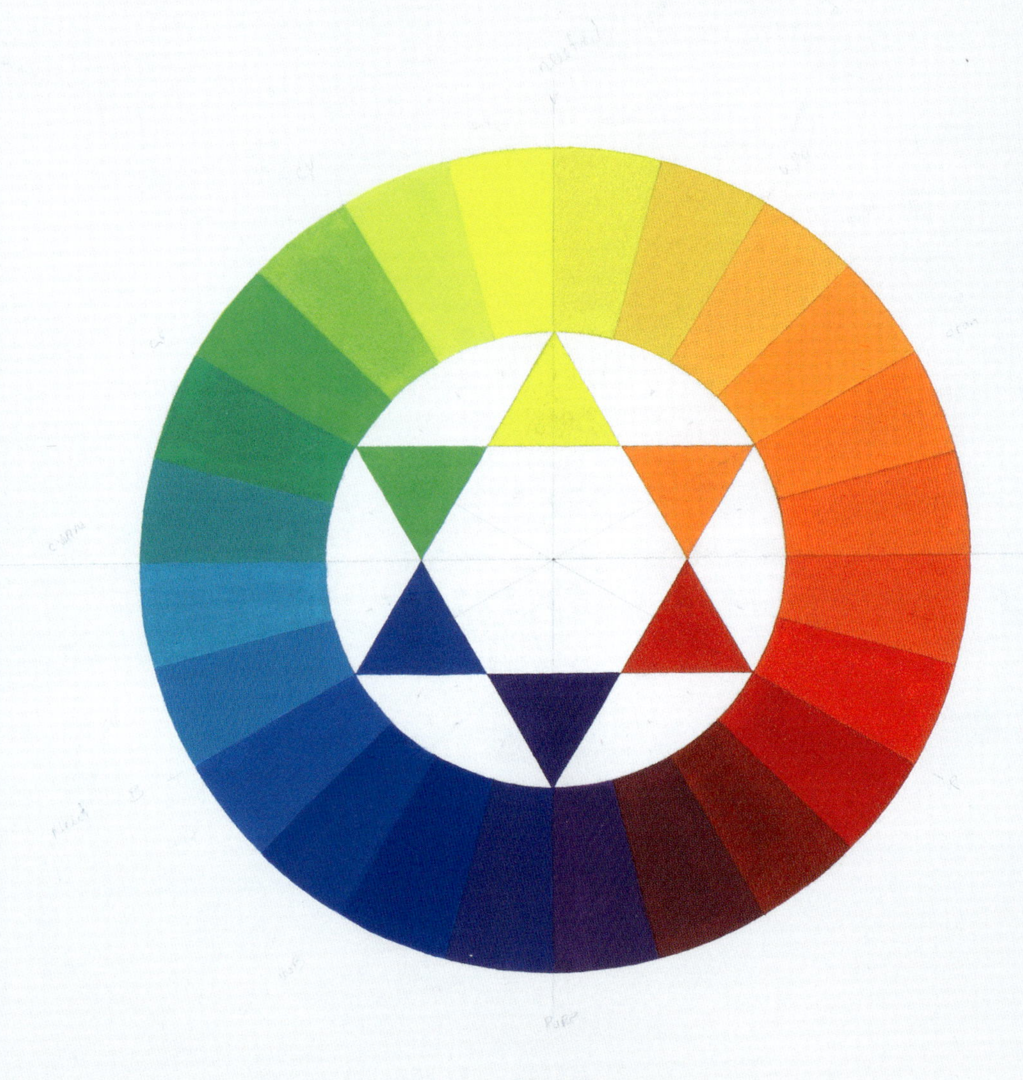

Introduction

In visual perception a colour is almost never seen as it really is – as it physically is. This fact makes colour the most relative medium in art.

Josef Albers, *Interaction of Color*

As I work on this book, my wife Michelle and I are redecorating the lounge. The walls were once a warm red, but we've decided it's time for a change. Anyone who's had to choose colours to redecorate a room knows what a nightmare this can be. The difference between the printed colour swatches from your local paint shop or DIY centre and the test samples on your walls quickly becomes apparent.

In fact, the sample pots are not only different to the printed samples, but they're also different on the walls when they're wet than when they're dry. They're different as a small square to how they are on a whole wall. They're different in morning light to evening light. They're different at night when the lights are on, and they're different in isolation to how they are next to other colours. They're even different when viewed at different angles. Colour truly is the most relative medium in art.

In this section, we'll be looking at how colours play together, how they interact with one another and how they visually mix. These principles can be used to inform the use of colour in your own work.

It is worth bearing in mind that the samples printed in this book will look different to how they are in real life and the colours you use may vary slightly from the ones I've used too. However, the principles will remain the same.

Volume *and* Weight

If you've ever heard someone say, 'They were wearing a loud shirt/dress', you may instantly get a mental image of someone wearing a very bright and unsubtle item of clothing. Conversely, if a colour is described as 'muted', you may understand the colour to be subtle and not very vibrant, turned down in terms of its visual impact. It might seem odd to talk about colour having a volume like sound, but I feel it can be a useful visual metaphor to explain certain colour interactions.

Colours interact like musical notes in an orchestra. The low bass notes are usually easier to listen to for prolonged periods, the mid-notes do most of the work and the high notes are put in for effect and in short bursts to save our sensitive hearing. Harmony is pleasing to hear, and dissonance is unsettling. In a way, colour is like this too. Subtle, muted colours are generally much easier to look at for long periods of time, whereas bright, intense colours might wake up the senses, but you probably wouldn't want your bedroom painted in them, or maybe you do!

This principle of colour volume plays a big part in pleasing colour combinations. Fully saturated purple and fully saturated yellow might be complementaries of one another, but they're pretty loud in combination. Let's look at some examples where the volume has been adjusted in each.

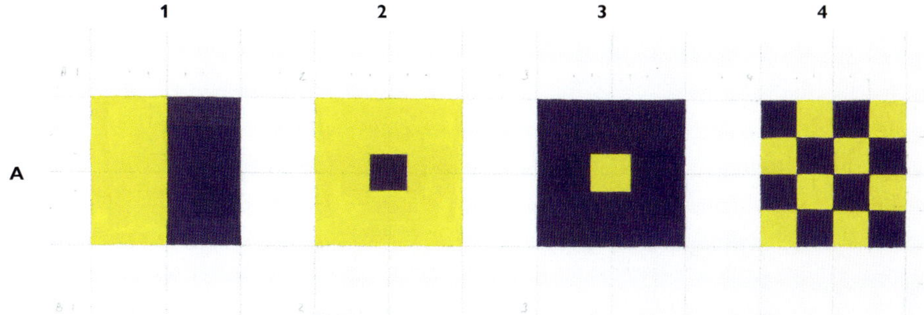

If we look at squares A2 and A3, the central square instantly grabs the attention like a single bold note, as the contrast between these two complementary colours is stark. One colour also has a smaller area compared to the larger area of the other, allowing the eye to see the central square easily and letting it get all the attention. I'll let you decide if one colour seems to recede and the other advances.

If we look at A1, we have equal areas of contrast, and the quantity of each colour is equal. They are easy to look at, but one colour doesn't stand out that much against the other, except in terms of value again. You could say that one is equally weighted against the other, to add another concept.

If you look at A4, however, the quantity of each colour is the same as A1; the contrast is the same, but the eye struggles to find a point to rest on and the image is less comfortable to look at, as if the colours are notes competing to be heard. Try repeating this exercise yourself and then try equalising the values like in C2 (see page 123).

With examples B1 and B3, both complementary colours have been muted by mixing the two together and adding a little white. Their values are very similar, making it much harder to differentiate one colour square from the other. To make the transition even smoother, I've added a second square around the central square of a value between that of the central and the surrounding outer square. This extra step in value is like adding a note between A and E on a piano to create a chord. I don't want to labour the musical similarities too much, but it's an interesting shared sensation.

Square B2 has had the purple of the central square mixed into the yellow of the outer square, but no white has been added. There's still an easier visual transition, but the perceived volume of the colours is louder and more noticeable. If you repeat this one yourself, try altering the value of the square between the central and outer ones by adding tiny and increasing amounts of purple to the yellow.

With C1, I've muted the colours and brought the values closer together by mixing the two complementary colours from A1 together. In C2, I've done the same and added white to tint them, plus I've equalised the values even more, making C2 the hardest to distinguish in terms of value. C3 is much the same as C2, but the values have been contrasted more. In C4, I've retained the saturation of the yellow by not adding purple but have softened it by adding a little white. In C5, the yellow is pure and the purple has been muted slightly by adding white, reducing the contrast and allowing the very dark purple to be more visible in terms of hue. Lastly, C6 has pure yellow, but the purple has been muted by adding some of the complementary yellow and white.

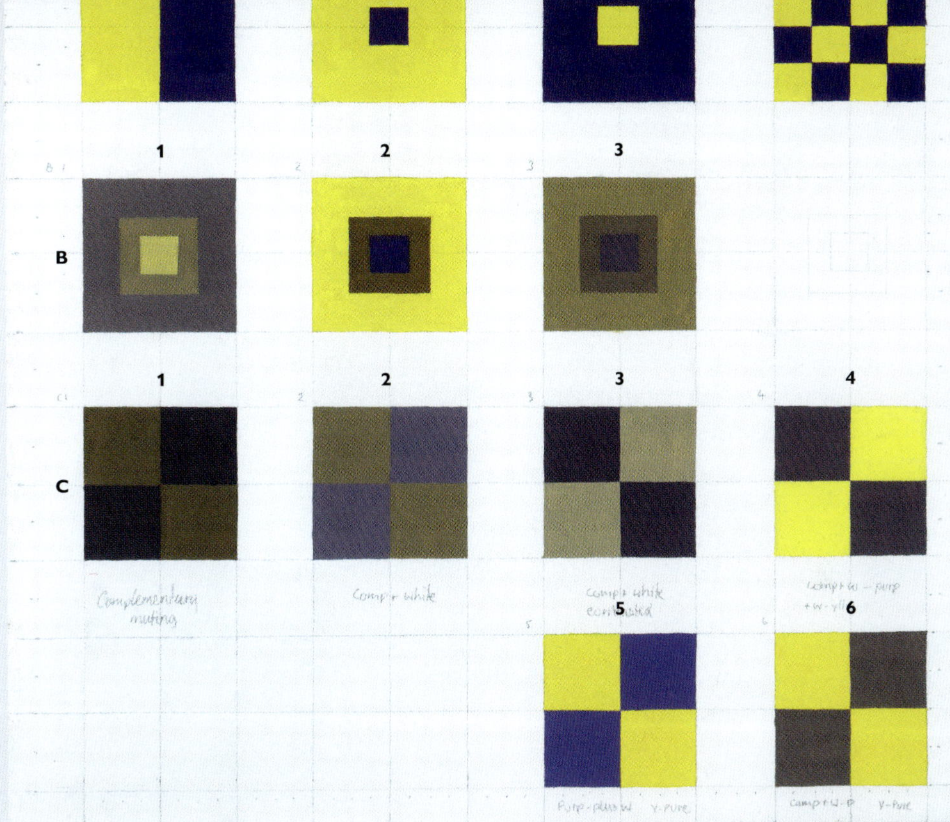

So, we can turn down, or up, the volume of a particular colour by varying the contrast of the colours around it. A pure colour will also stand out more against a muted colour. Try adding the complementary, or a little white, to one of the colours in A2 and A3 and see what you think. However, if the values are the same, the contrast is lost and one colour can disappear next to the other, which can occasionally be very handy, especially if you want to use a very bold colour among muted colours of the same value.

Let's look at some more examples on the following pages.

A1 and B1 show just about the most extreme examples of contrast that you can create: a small square against a large volume of the opposite value. C1 has had the value of the outer square reduced by adding white and creating a mid-grey. The white still stands out, but not as much as in B1. D1 has the same grey as C1, but the central square is now a grey similar in value to the outer square, making it extremely difficult to see.

If you look at row 2, I've repeated the experiment of row 1 but used the yellow and purple again, rather than black and white. The values are mirroring those of row 1, except in D2, where I've muted the outer square with white a little more to drop the value to get closer to the pure yellow in the centre.

Row 3 is all obvious complementary pairs, except A3 and B3, where I've only used one colour but muted the value of the outer square by adding a little of the complementary purple.

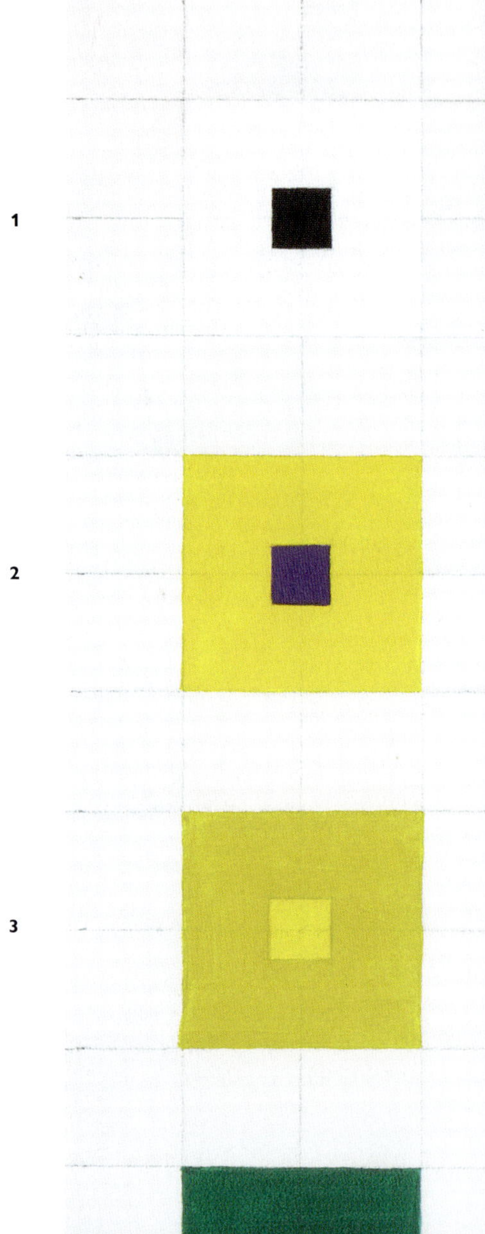

B
C
D

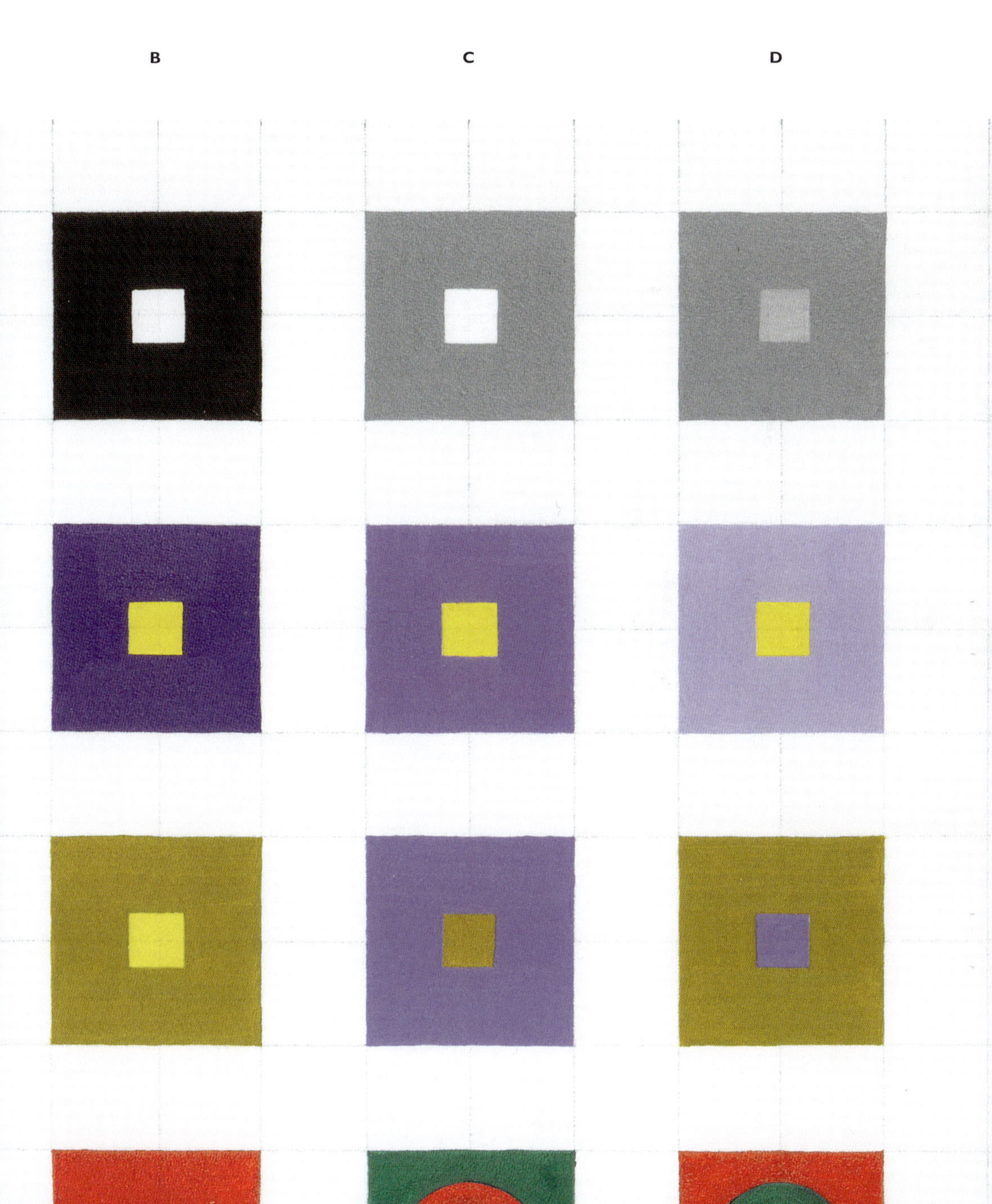

Note how hard it is to look at row 4, where the values and saturation of each colour are almost the same. Do you think the circles in C4 and D4 seem to add to visual confusion? If you push the values of the examples on this strip further apart, they will be much easier on the eye and brain. If your aim is to induce a sort of visual nausea, try pairing colours at full saturation and identical values.

Rows 5 and 6 are a variety of tints and full-saturation combinations of orange and blue complementary examples for you to think about. Again, try taking a pair of complementary colours, or any colours, and try repeating these squares in varying combinations of values, tints, tones, shades and neutrals.

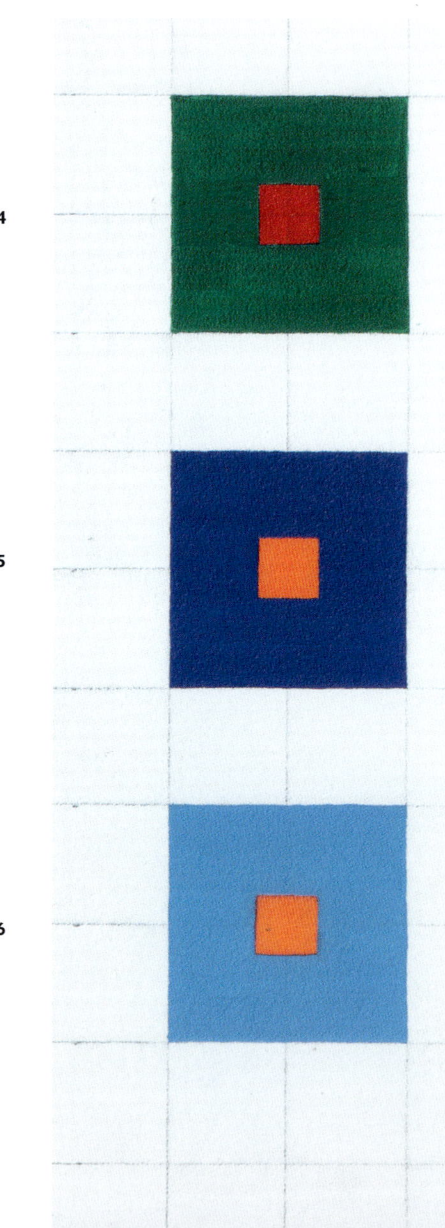

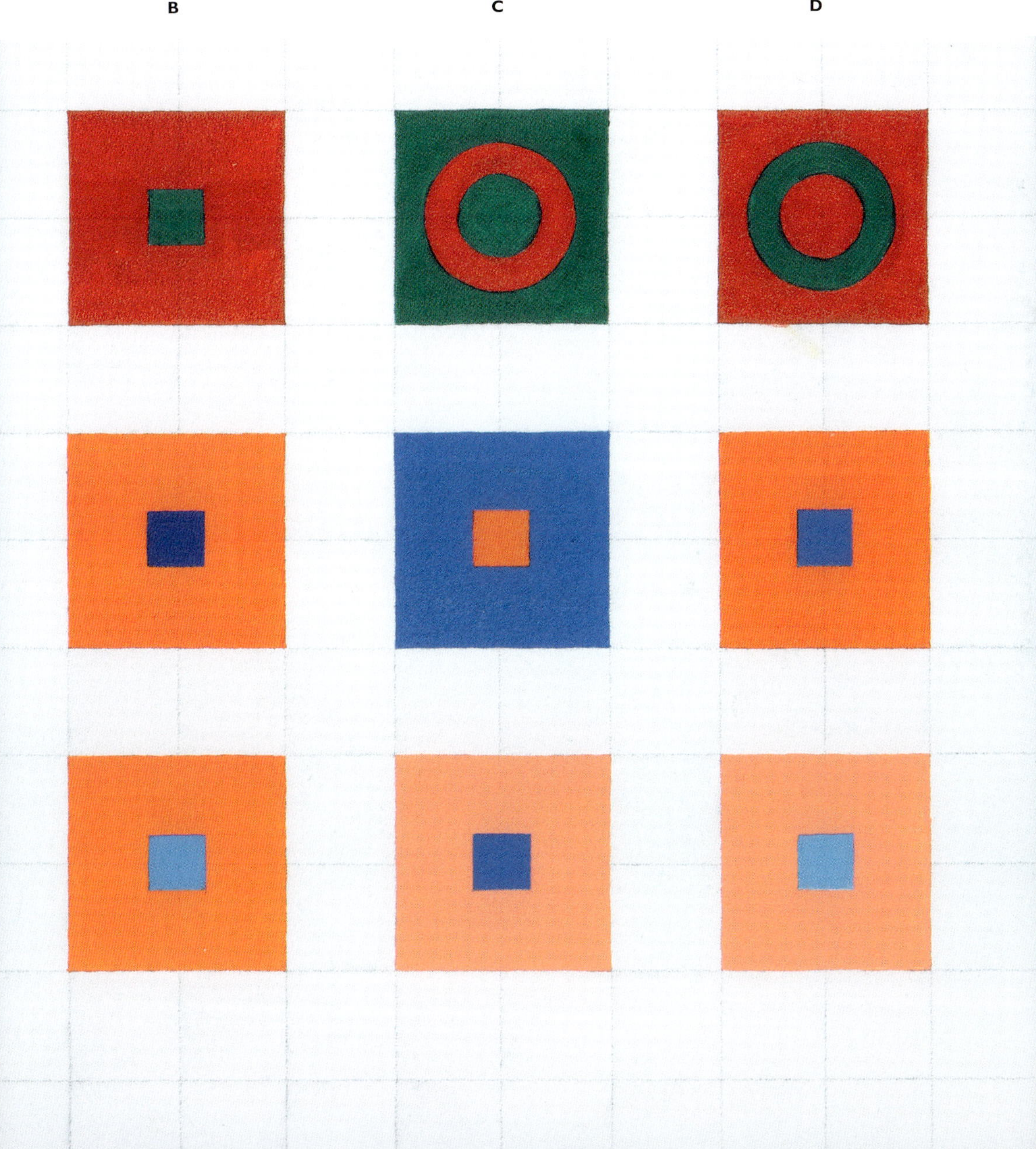

B
C
D

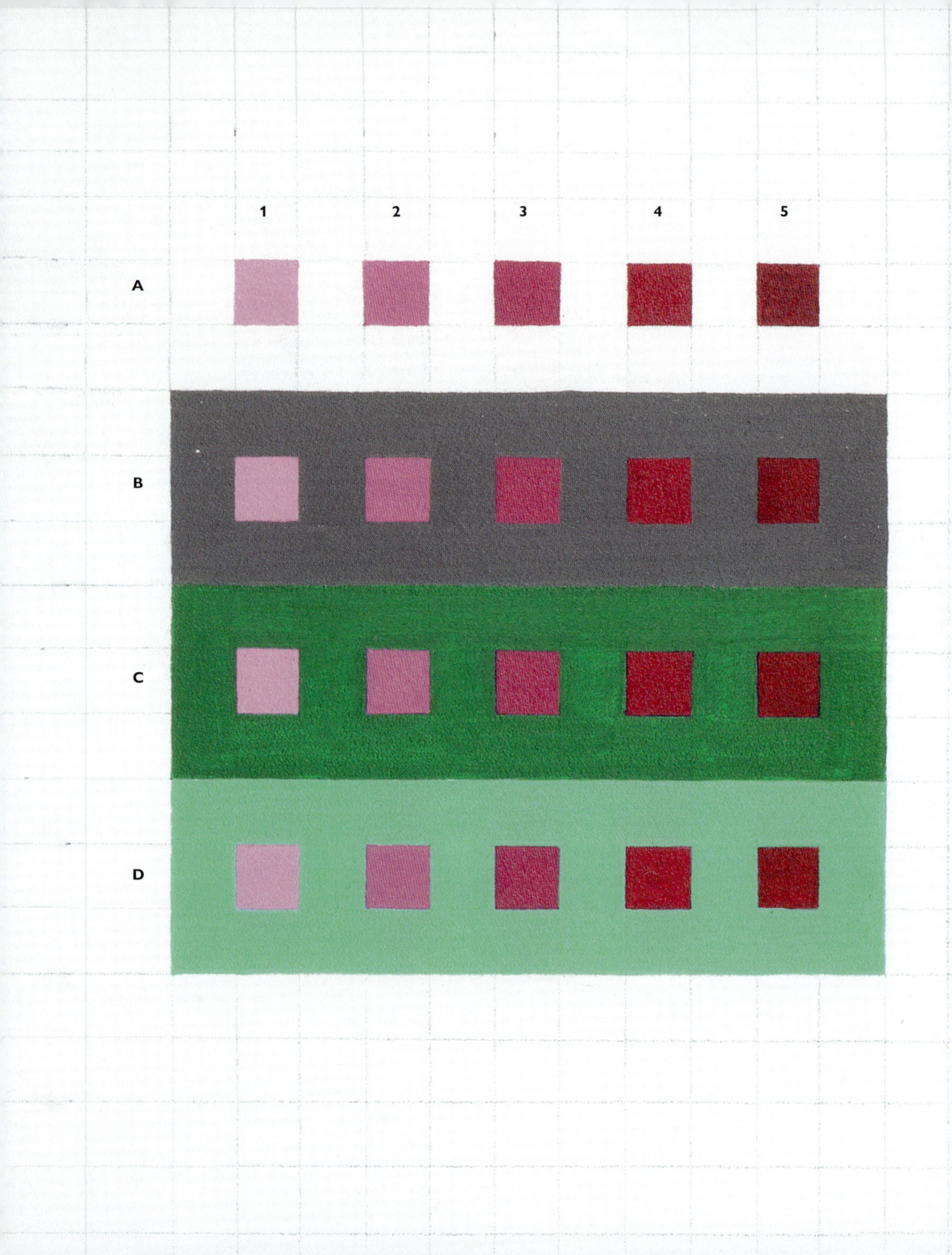

1 2 3 4 5
A
B
C
D

Contrast is the greatest factor in building the illusion of form in a painting – without it, there is no shadow, no highlight, no mid-tones, no form. Look at the squares opposite.

In row A, there are five examples of magenta in five differing values, from light to dark. If you insert this strip into mid-grey, as in row B, the lightest and darkest values stand out the most, whereas square 3 practically disappears, as its value is so close to its surroundings.

Row C is similar, but this time we have the complementary colour of magenta at a similar value to row B. Again, square 3 wants to blend into its surroundings, plus the addition of colour makes things even more confusing around some squares.

In Row D, the square with the value closest to the lighter-tinted background of green is the hardest to see. It's the contrast that makes one colour stand out against another; hue can enhance this, but it's contrast that provides form and the illusion of depth.

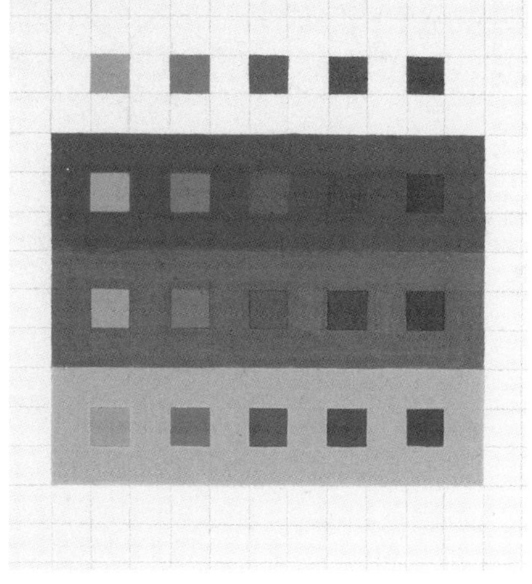

Left This is a monochrome version of the diagram on the page opposite. When the colours are removed, it is even easier to see which squares are closest in value.

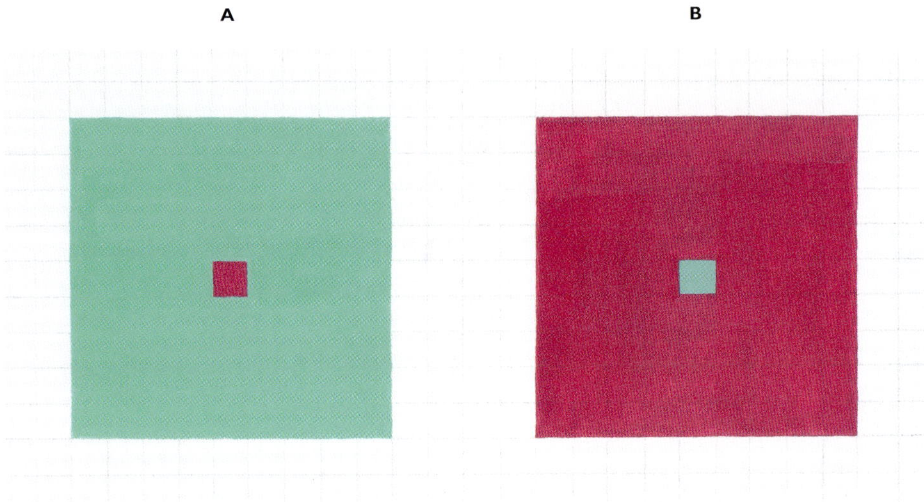

Finally, look at squares A and B above. Square A has a large volume of a green tint and a small magenta square in the centre; square B has the reverse. Both have good contrast, but which seems heavier? Would you say one has a greater sense of weight? Not only does the size of the small square make it much more interesting against the much larger square, but the value of each square seems to give the impression of weight too. Darker colours seem to feel heavier than lighter colours. The fact that each small square is surrounded by its complementary is adding to the visual punch of the small square, but the size and particularly the value of each square seems to have a weight to it. This is perhaps because we associate shadows with being larger and at the base of many objects, and highlights being smaller and near the top of an object. Whatever the reason, darker colours seem heavier than lighter-value colours, don't you think?

To finish, here are six more squares using the complementary colours orange and blue in various values, tints, tones and shades. All the colours you see here are mixed from combinations of the same orange and blue, with white occasionally being added.

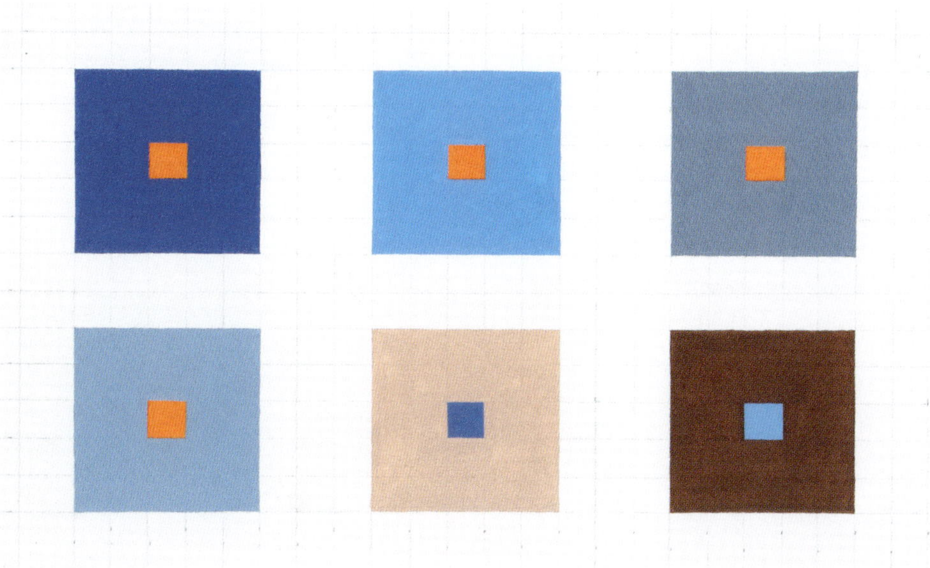

Transitions *and* Form

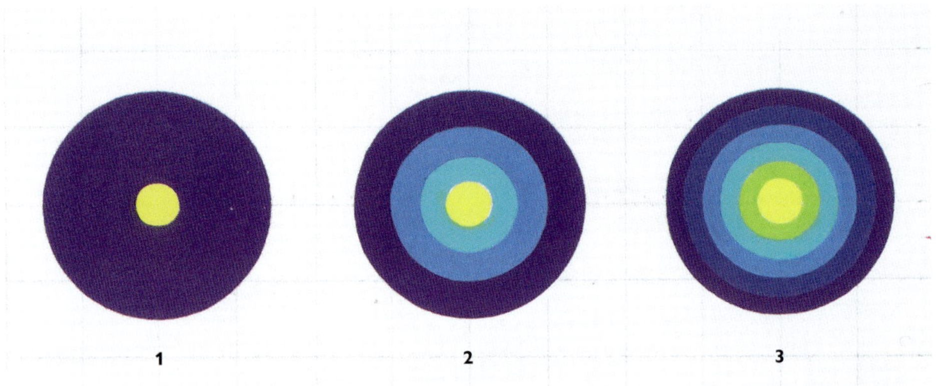

Our eyes are constantly roaming across objects in our field of vision and often use edges to make sense of the world around us. Sharp changes in the values we see indicate depth or an edge, whereas a gradual change will suggest a curve. We can use colours to mimic the way in which our eyes interpret edges to show transition and volume.

In the diagram above, we have a purple circle with a yellow dot in the centre. The dot seems to be isolated from the purple background, much

like a star in the night sky. If we begin to add extra rings and make their values transitional, making each one slightly darker from yellow to purple (2), the dot no longer seems so isolated. If we add yet more circles (3) and transitions, your eyes are now ranging across these subtle changes and beginning to suggest this shape might have three dimensions. In these three circles, I've used colours that roughly follow the natural value order of the spectrum.

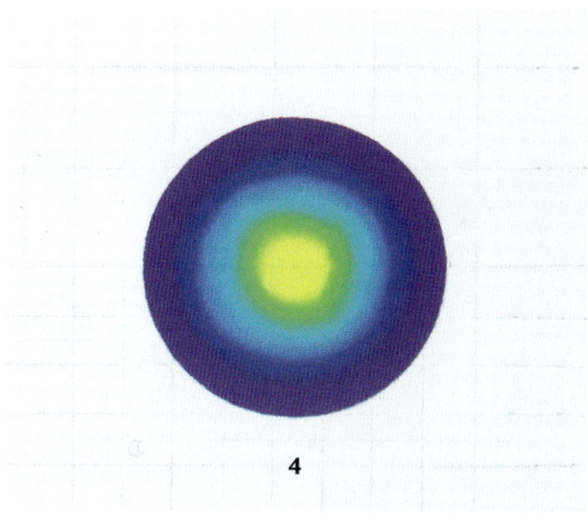

4

In the illustration below, I've used red and added white to tint the red and black (although its complementary 'green' might have been a better value modifier) to shade it. The colour is at peak saturation around the central line. This Goldilocks point (A) is where light isn't beginning to wash it out and shadow isn't beginning to mute it, but notice how much the transitions of value (and the elliptical lines) are suggesting a three-dimensional shape. Were you to blur the edges of the transitions, it would increase the illusion of a ball. Edges stop the eye while blurred areas encourage it to keep moving.

If we take circle 3 and blend the edges of those transitions to create a visual blur (4), the circle looks even more three-dimensional. If we tip the rings in the circle and make them slightly elliptical, the image will look very much like a ball.

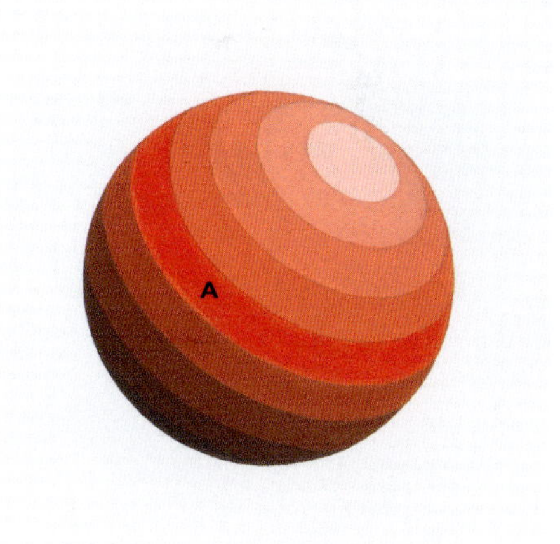

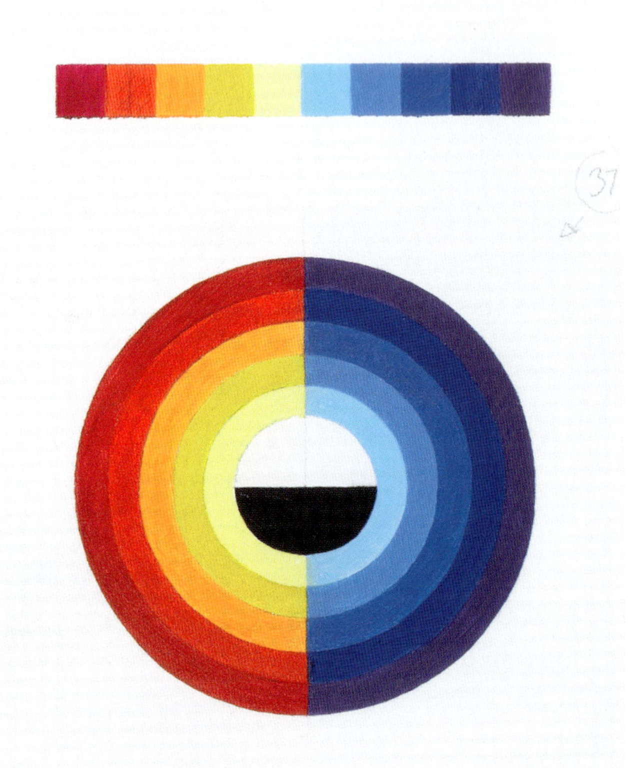

The spectrum in the diagram above is split in half. I've taken out green as a sort of neutral zone in the centre and placed the warm side on the left and the cool on the right, in the order you would expect to see the colours on the spectrum. Seen like this, you can clearly see an order of value in the colours. If we apply them roughly to a couple of spheres, that order of values in the colours naturally gives us the order of values in the form too. With the blue sphere, I've included the dark red from the other side of purple on the spectrum to suggest reflected light.

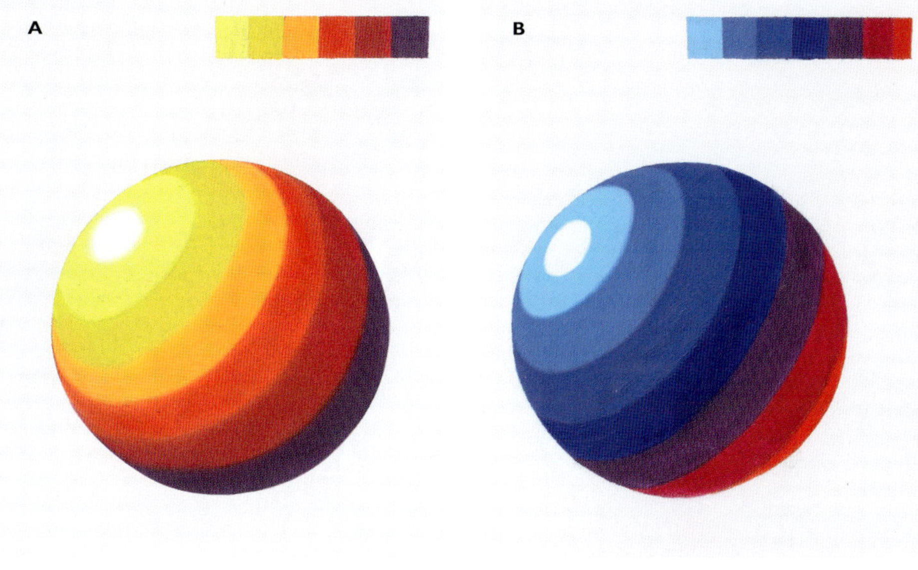

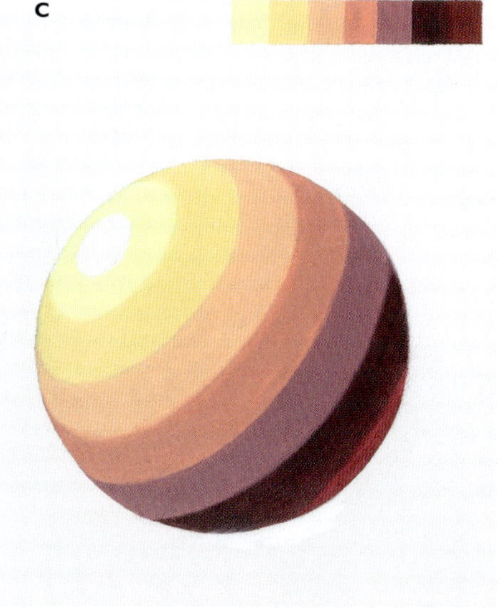

So, you see how these transitions of value suggest form. Of course, they don't have to be done in spectrum colours, I just thought it a useful illustration to show how the spectrum colours seem to naturally follow an order of values.

A Form suggested using the values of warm spectrum hues

B Form suggested using the values of cool spectrum hues

C Muted version of A with white added to the colours to create a range of tints

I used a few photos I'd taken that showed marked colour transitions as examples on which to base the colour studies shown below. Each colour study has the two colours concerned side by side, but in column A, I've mixed the two colours and added a central bar as a transitional colour from one to the other. The three examples in column B have sharp boundaries, especially where the values differ a lot, but the examples in column A seem to blend into one another more naturally.

In column C, I used a photo of my face as a reference. The pink on the left is similar to my skin tone and the brown is a shadow cast by my nose. The reddish-brown bar in the centre is the transitional colour seen between those two colours. In the first image, I've made the transitional bar wider, the second is narrower but still there, and the last is just the two colours side by side. These transitional values/colours are often overlooked but are essential for rendering a realistic image. They're also beautiful in their own right, of course, and have a huge range of design applications.

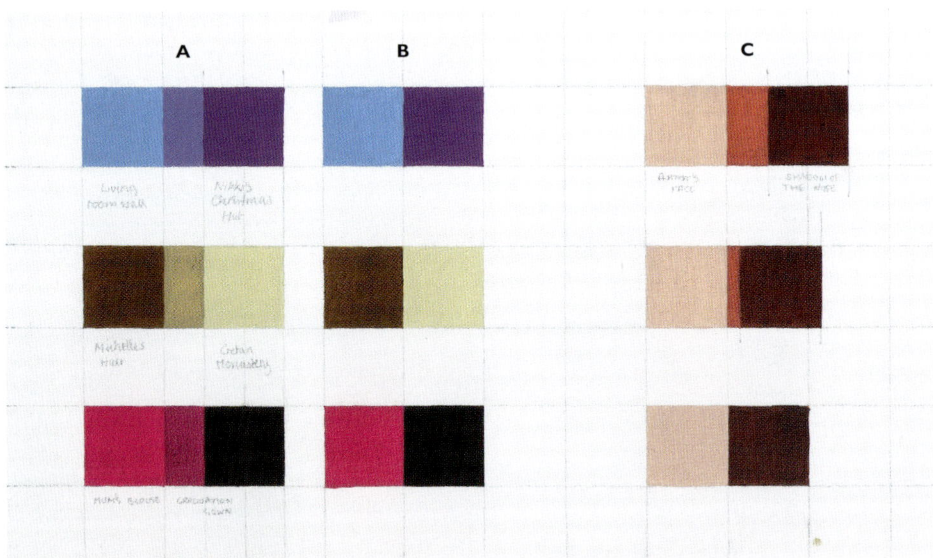

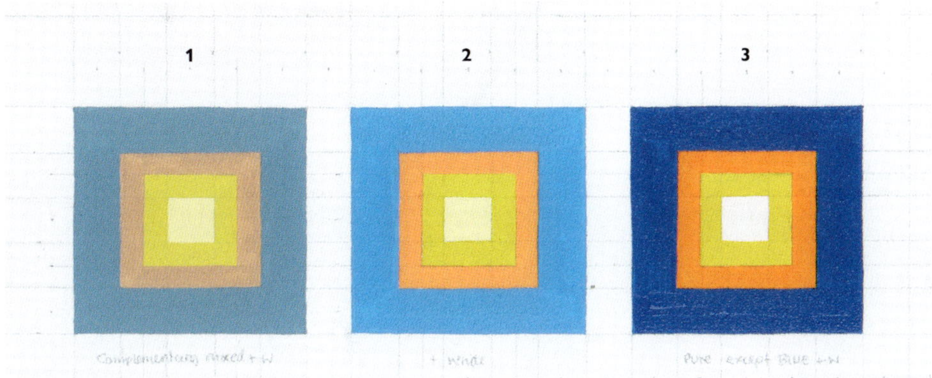

In the three examples above, we can see complementary pairs (orange and blue), with the orange being given two extra values and colour transitions. Note how the image immediately suggests depth by adding successional values. Example 3 is using full-saturation colours (although the phthalocyanine blue (PB15:1) has had some white added so you can see it). Example 2 uses the colours from example 3 but are tinted by the addition of white, and example 1 has had the blue added to the orange and yellow, and orange added to the blue to decrease the saturation (these colours have also been tinted with white to mute them further and equalise the values). The muting of the colours has visually softened the edges, as the values are less pronounced, and made the image less distinct. Equalising, or reducing the difference in values, also reduces the sense of form.

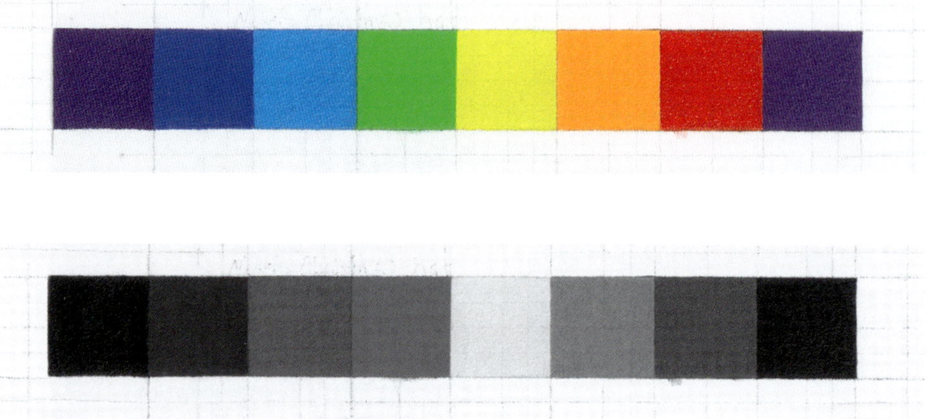

Take a look at the strip above of
the full-saturation painted spectrum
colours. Each one of these colours has
its own inherent value. The yellow
is almost 100% white, the warm red
would be somewhere around the
middle of the value scale, maybe
50%, and the purple would be almost
100% black.

You can see this more clearly in
the black-and-white version below it.

Now, if you take one of those spectrum colours and try to equalise the values of all the other colours to it, all of the perceived depth provided by the difference in values of those colours would more or less disappear. In the image above, I've taken orange as our reference point, kept it all full saturation and tried to match the values of all the other colours to it. This turned out to be difficult, but hopefully you can see from the black-and-white version below it that I got pretty close.

If you try to repeat this exercise and use yellow as your unchanged colour and try to equalise the values of all the other colours to it, all the other hues will look almost white and only the yellow will be a clear colour, as yellow is almost 100% white in terms of value. Warm red would be somewhere around 50% grey in terms of value, and purple would be almost 100% black. So, using red would result in a lot of mid-tone colours, and if you use purple, it will be difficult to see any of the other mixed colours, as they'd be so dark. Why not pick a colour and try it yourself?

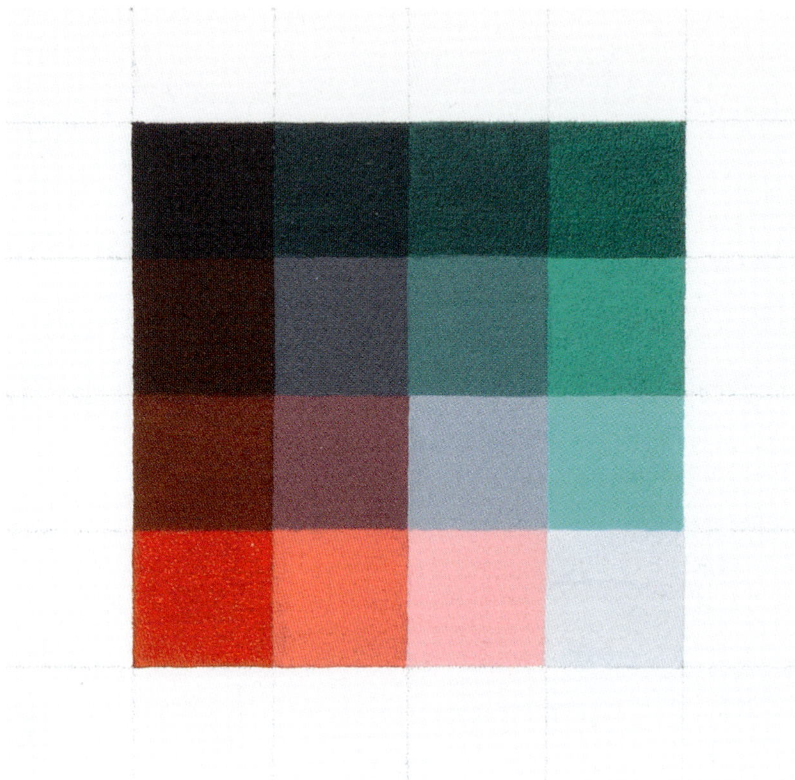

This is why single-value pictures are extremely hard to paint, as only one colour will be at full saturation, all the others will be tints, tones or shades of that colour depending on its value, and there will be almost no visible depth to the image at all. If, however, you matched the values of the image you wanted to paint to the inherent full-saturation values of the spectrum colours, you would have a painting with plenty of depth and form, but it would be eye-achingly loud!

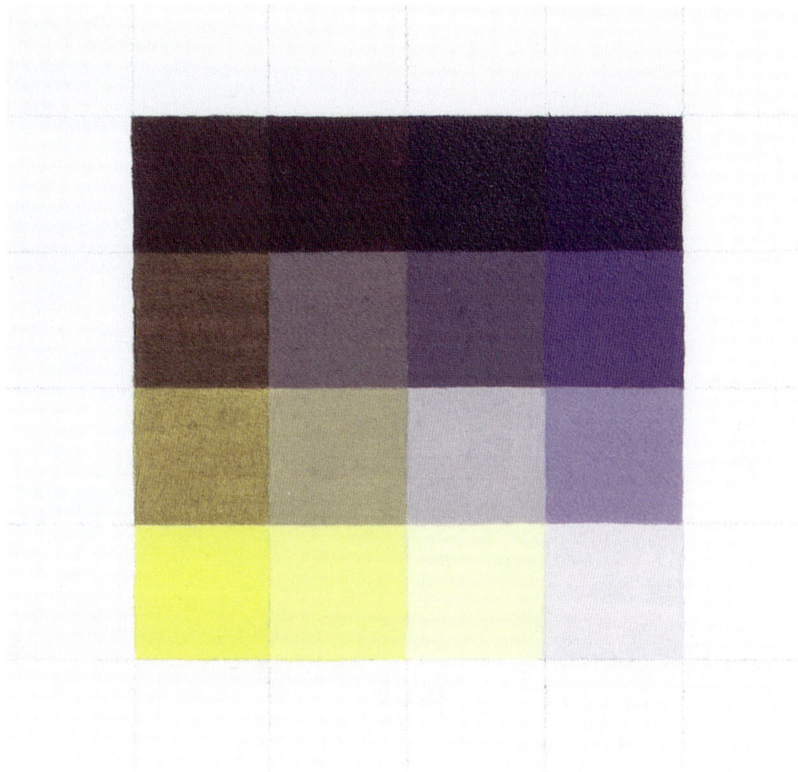

Each of these illustrations is a mix of one primary and its complementary, which is why they mix a diagonal row of neutrals. The top-right and bottom-left squares are the only pure colours. White has been added to make the tints in the right-hand column, in increasing increments from top to bottom. The bottom row has had the same white added to make a row of tints from left to right. Then each column has been added incrementally to the corresponding row, until the mixes reach neutrality in the diagonal from top left to bottom right.

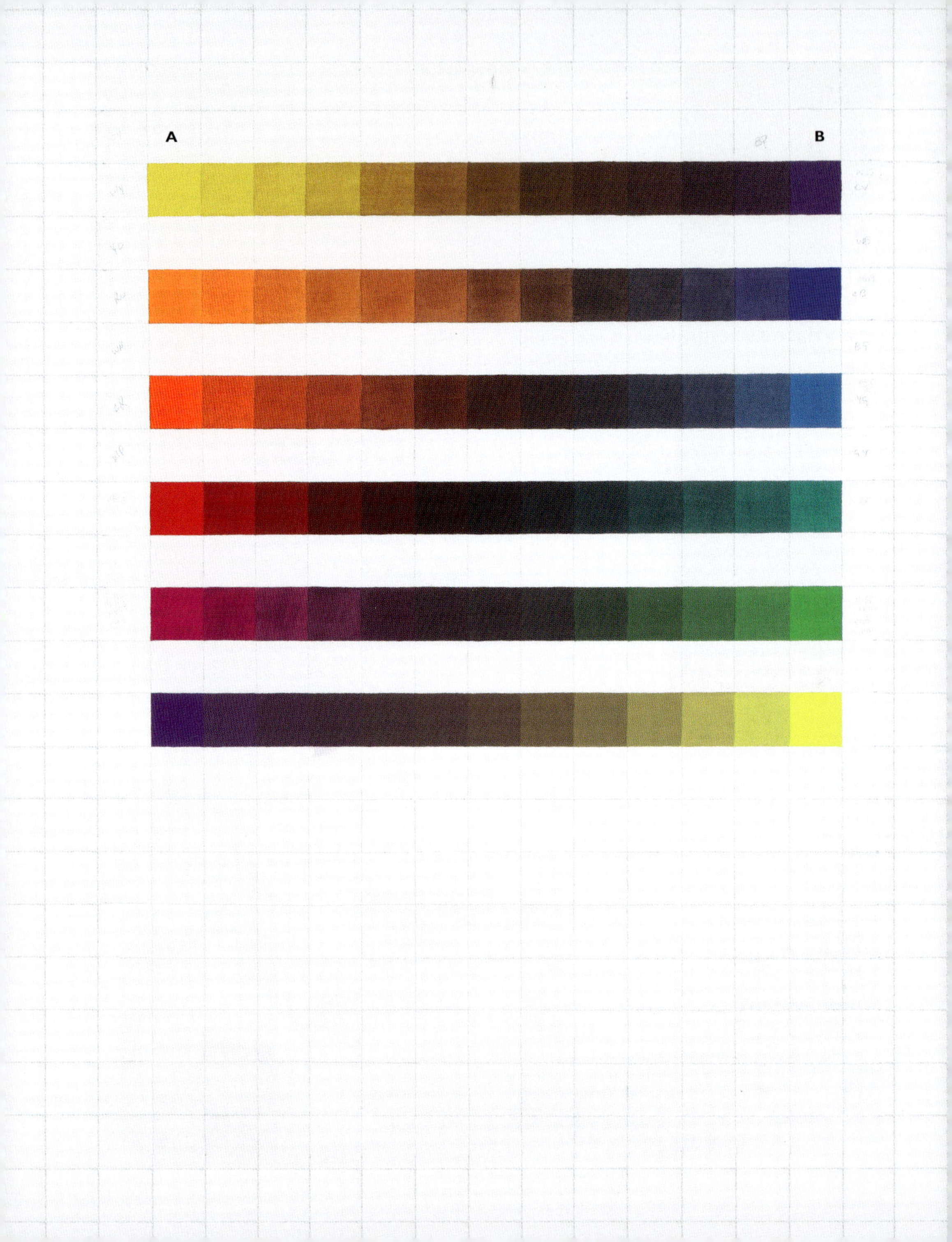

A
B

In the diagram opposite, A is added incrementally to B in each case, altering the value and, by default, the saturation. Note how the relative darkness or lightness of each colour affects the range of available values. Also note how two mid-value colours (red and green here) reach their darkest value and complete colour neutrality in the centre of the range, whereas the darkest and lightest colours do this at the ends of the top and bottom rows, making a neat diagonal of dark values across the diagram.

Notice how often in real life the lighter-value spectrum colours, such as yellow or cyan, are found in highlights, where purple and deep blue are found in the shadows (because of the extremity of the values of these colours, they can be hard to see clearly in a real-world situation). If in doubt, always refer to the order you would expect to see in the spectrum. If your eye gets tuned in to noticing these spectrum-order transitions, you'll start to see them all over the place – in halos around lights, colours in a flame, gradients of colour in a shadow on a bright day, the subtle transitions of light in snow. Reproducing colours well is 98% good observation guided by 2% of what you know to be true scientifically, but in times of doubt, remember that 2% can often save the day.

5

Pigments *and* Paints

The Nature *of* Paint

This is really a book about colour as opposed to paint, but since nearly every example is painted in artists' oil colours, it feels important to write a little about the nature of paint itself. The reason I got into studying colour, and I am sure this is true of many artists, was to help me mix paint better.

Paint is essentially a coloured powder that has a binder added to it. The binder – a substance that holds all the pigment particles together to make a paste or liquid – can vary, but it is the binder that allows the paint to exist in a liquid form that will, once applied, hopefully dry to create a solid film of colour. For watercolour, the added binder will be a natural gum, extracted from a tree, which dissolves with water; for acrylic, an acrylic polymer; for oil paint, linseed oil, safflower oil or some other usually natural oil that dries reliably. The paint used almost exclusively in the illustrations in this book is oil paint, but the principles remain the same for any paint colour.

1 Pigment
The coloured dust that gives the paint its colour.

2 Binder
The substance that holds all the pigment particles together to make a paste or liquid form of colour.

3 Other ingredients
The elements added to paint that manufacturers are sometimes a little shy about sharing. They can include fillers, wetting agents and other chemicals.

The pigment is the most important
ingredient in any paint, as the source
of the colour. It is often also what
dictates the price of the colour: the
more expensive pigments are those
that are rare, difficult to manufacture
or expensive to manufacture. Some
pigments are difficult to manufacture
but are so widely used in industrial
production that the price is low, for
instance phthalocyanine blue (PB15),
which is used in car paint and the dying
of jeans. When pigments are difficult
to manufacture and used almost
exclusively by a relatively small group of
artists, the price is usually much higher.

If two colours say they contain the
same pigment but have vastly differing
prices, this could be because one
manufacturer bulks out the pigment
with other substances, but it could also
be as simple and innocent as savings
made by the manufacturer purchasing
the pigment at scale. The only way to
tell a paint's quality regarding your own
usage is to try it out. It is also worth
noting that some manufacturers can
make a range of wonderful paints and a
couple of awful ones, or a range of bad
paints and a couple of fantastic-value
ones, so shop around.

The binder in artists' oil paint is
usually a plant oil (although I made
some with motor oil once and they still
haven't dried!). Plant-based oil paints
dry well and produce a strong film of
paint. Linseed oil probably makes the
most durable binder, but safflower
is very useful in colours that would
be affected by yellowing, such as the
paler cool colours and white, as linseed
can yellow the colours a little over
time. Poppy oil and walnut oil are also
popular choices, but linseed is the oil in
most artists' colours and rarely causes
any problems. A good-quality binder
will contribute greatly to a good-
quality, long-lasting paint.

The other ingredients are those you're unlikely to see listed on the labels of *any* artists' paint colours, but I hope we will one day. In general, colours using bad fillers are very easy to spot compared to good-quality paint. They are likely to mix less-vibrant, greyish colours, and may produce poor glazes when thinned, or simply have very little tinting ability.

Conversely, some fillers aren't used to save money at all and can actually be more expensive than the pigment. Some are necessary to suppress separation of the pigment and binder in the tube. Some can also be very useful for formulating some colours that, if used on their own, would need more body/structure.

Below is a far-from-exhaustive list of 'other ingredients' you might find in artists' oil colours:

1. **Barium sulphate**. One of the commonest and cheapest fillers. An inert, dense, white-and-crystalline substance that improves volume, opacity, consistency and viscosity of paint. Also used to add weight to the tube of paint. Some manufacturers use synthetic barium sulphate (or sulfate) as a filler, but it occurs naturally as the mineral barite.

2. **Aluminium hydrate/trihydrate/ aluminium hydroxide.** A white/ translucent filler, extender and bulking agent also found commercially in fire extinguishers. Sometimes used as a base for synthetic pigments such as phthalocyanine blue or green.

3. **Aluminium stearate.** Aluminium distearate is a white-coloured powder and is the most used grade of aluminium stearate. It is used as a thickener in paints, transforming oil paint into a gel, and imparts that 'buttery' consistency. It also helps prevent separation of pigment from oil in the tube.

Pigments *and* Paints

4. **Mica (hydrous aluminium potassium silicate).** Mostly used in glittery paint and cosmetics.

5. **Calcite/calcium carbonate.** Chalk, a bulking agent.

6. **Marble dust.** Bulking agent.

7. **Driers.** Such as cobalt.

8. **Koalin/china clay.** A white, chalky clay that helps prevent oil and pigment separating.

8. **Wax/beeswax.** Used for bulking and giving paint that 'buttery' look.

10. **Glass powder.** Gives luminosity to colour.

11. **Surfactants.** Detergents used as wetting agents to help pigment bond to oil.

12. **Carboxylic acid (salts).** Used as wetting agents.

13. **Zinc stearate.** A water repellent and preservative.

I'd love to see manufacturers print all ingredients on their paint labels. I understand why they're hesitant to do this though, because artists are understandably suspicious of 'other ingredients' in their paint, and some manufacturers play on this by advertising their colours as having nothing but pigment and oil in them. But some of the 'other ingredients' are essential in getting some pigments to bind to the oil, or to bulk out the pigment enough to make a buttery paste rather than a puddle of colour when it's squeezed out of the tube.

We should also consider whether the paint we buy comes from ethically mined or produced pigments. If every manufacturer was upfront about the ingredients in their paint, we could compare brands and make up our own minds about where to shop. The more open and honest the manufacturer is, the more inclined I am to buy from them or endorse their products.

If you were to play the old 'animal, vegetable or mineral?' guessing game, the answer for pigment could be just 'yes'. Some pigment is made from plants (for example, alizarin crimson), some from burnt animal bones (such as ivory black), some from earth minerals (the umbers) and some from metals such as cadmium, iron and zinc. Some even have the same name and are the same colour but are made from different substances. Colours that imitate genuine pigments have 'hue' after their name, but don't be lured into thinking that because they're not the genuine item in terms of pigment, they're not as good in terms of colour; some are better, some are worse and some depend on the application.

Pigment is essentially a substance that has been smashed, pulverised and milled on a machine until it's a dust comprised of microscopic particles in a variety of very fine <0.3µm to very coarse >40µm sizes ('very coarse' is a little misleading, as it's still no bigger than a grain of very fine sand). However, even after it's been smashed to microscopic pieces, the pigment will still be different in nature, even though it's tiny.

Imagine you have a pile of straw, a pile of glass and a pile of mud, and you do your best to smash each pile to dust; the pieces of each pile will differ greatly from one another. The pile of plant material might look like dry compost, the glass might look like a broken window or shattered windscreen, and the mud might be clumpy, but you'd easily be able to see the difference in their nature. Were they to get ground to dust to make pigment, their nature still wouldn't change a great deal, they'd just be much smaller pieces. In terms of longevity, plant-based dust is more delicate than metallic or mineral dust. Also, each microscopic particle will look different and have a different surface.

Pigment particles can be (to name but a few shapes and types) rounded, angular, thin, tubular, shell-like, rough, pitted, opaque, transparent, fibrous, crystalline, smooth, prismatic or a combination of any of these. The shape and surface of each pigment particle will affect the way in which light is reflected from it, or through it, and how much oil (binder) it will absorb, due to how large its surface area is or how porous it is.

As I'm not an artists' paint-maker, I thought it might be helpful to give you a viewpoint on the subject from someone who is.

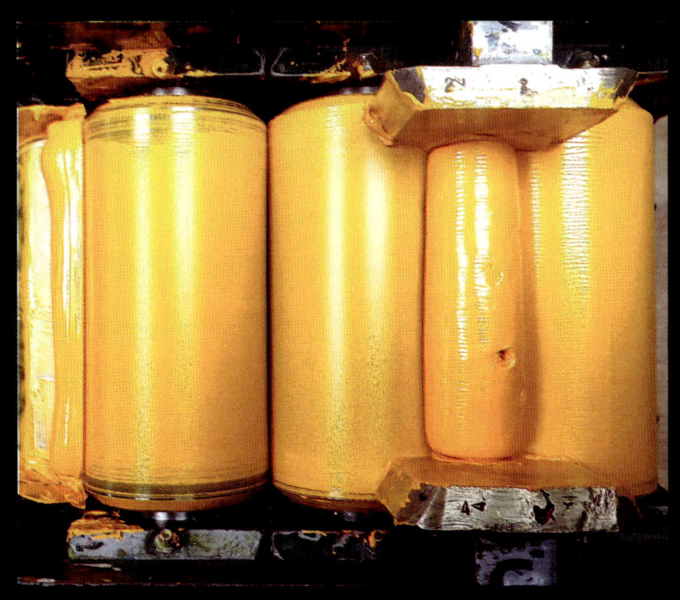

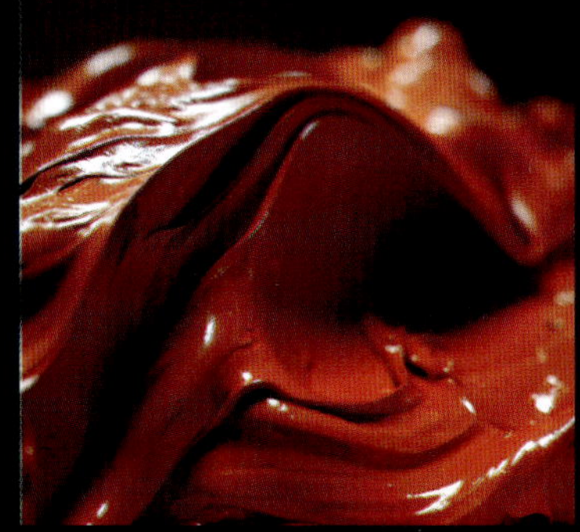

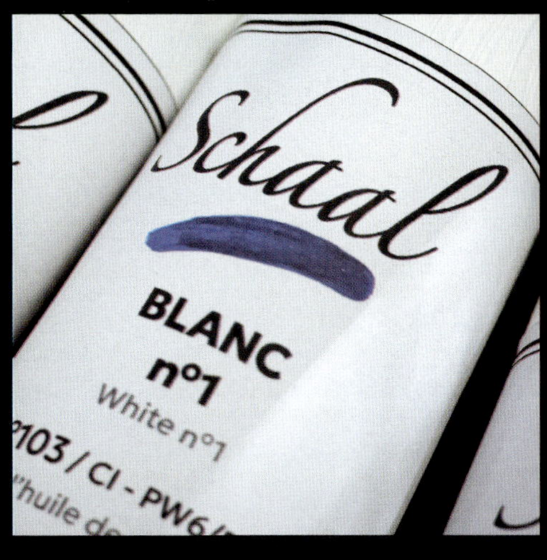
Schaal
BLANC
n°1
White n°u
n°103 / CI - PW6/
d'huile de

On Making Paint

My friend François Schaal, a quality paint-maker, has shared some of his experience on creating paint. According to him, the oil requirements needed to mix paint from certain pigments can sometimes even exceed 100%, such as ivory black. Below are some oil percentages for certain pigments:

> Lead white: about 13% oil
> Titanium white: 18–22%
> Cobalt blue: 20–30%
>   (cerulean 15–25%)
> Ultramarine blue: 31–36%
> Cadmium yellow: about 20%
> Titanium nickel yellow: 14–18%
> Yellow ochre: 30–40%
> Cadmium red: about 20%
> Green earth: about 80%
> Sienna: about 80%
> Burnt sienna: about 60%
> Lamp black: 80–100%
> Ivory black: 80–110%

In terms of density, this varies a great deal as well. The weights of some pigments in grams per cubic centimetre are as follows:

> Titanium white: 4.26 g/cm^3
> Yellow ochre: 3.49–4.30 g/cm^3
> Green earth: 2.79 g/cm^3
> Cobalt blue: 2.35 g/cm^3
> Ultramarine violet: 2.35 g/cm^3
> Prussian blue: 1.83 g/cm^3

Transparent colours are completely different from opaque colours because they are less dense and more complex to disperse and grind. One of the pigments that requires the least oil is lead white because its density is very high compared to, say, a French green earth.

There are always exceptions when you take into account the nature of the pigment and its reaction when it is crushed and milled. In general, with earth colours, we can make around thirty to thirty-five tubes of paint, more or less, from a kilo of pigment. For an alizarin crimson, I can make up to forty to forty-five tubes, and for a lead white, barely fifteen tubes. Genuine naples yellow can sometimes only yield nine tubes, so the density of the pigment plays a big part in how it mixes with the oil and therefore how much paint can be made from each kilo of pigment.

Pigments are not all physically the same. The example opposite is a natural yellow ochre made from crushed rock (PY43), and on the next page is a synthetic yellow ochre (PY42). You can see that the synthetically manufactured pigment comprises smaller particles than the pigment made from crushed rock. Natural yellow ochre is often much grittier than the synthetic equivalent. I prefer PY42, but another artist might prefer the rougher PY43 – the same colour, but different pigment particles.

This gives you an insight into the physical nature of paint and the differences in the pigment as a physical substance, but what about the much more important job of conveying colour to the viewer?

Each of those tiny pigment particles will reflect or absorb light differently and affect the levels of light and colour reflected back to the viewer. Some, such as the transparent colours, will let light pass through them and bounce off the surface underneath the paint, while others, such as the opaque colours, reflect light primarily from a dense surface of colour. However, this can have little bearing on their value in terms of lightness and darkness.

A microscope can give us an insight into the physical nature of paint and the differences in the pigment as a physical substance.

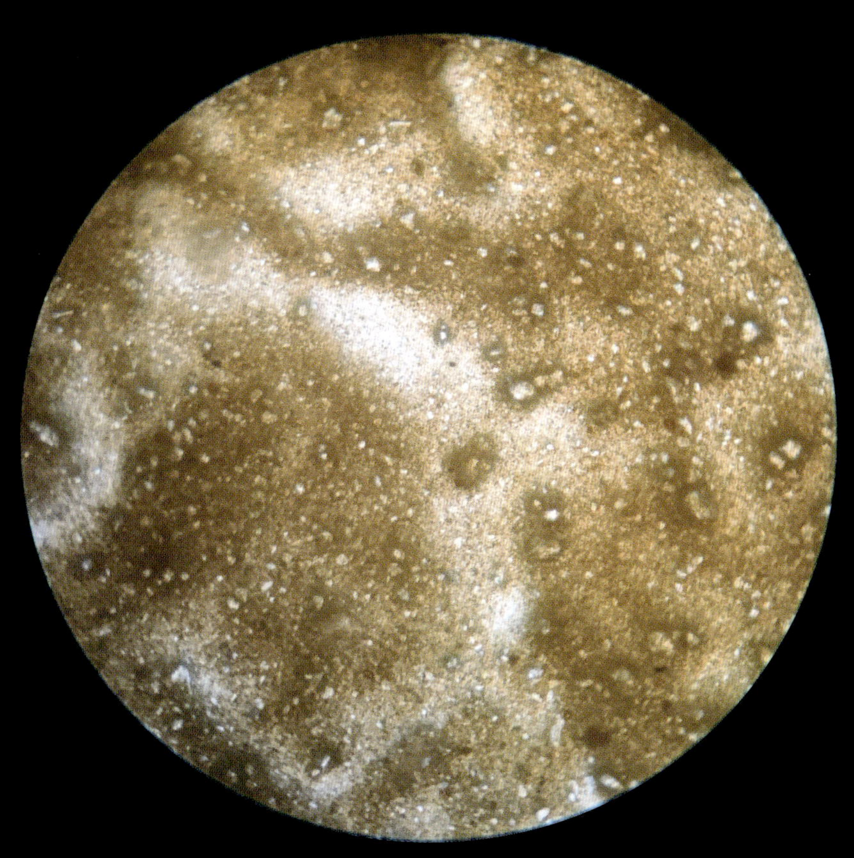

PY43
NATURAL
YELLOW
OCHRE

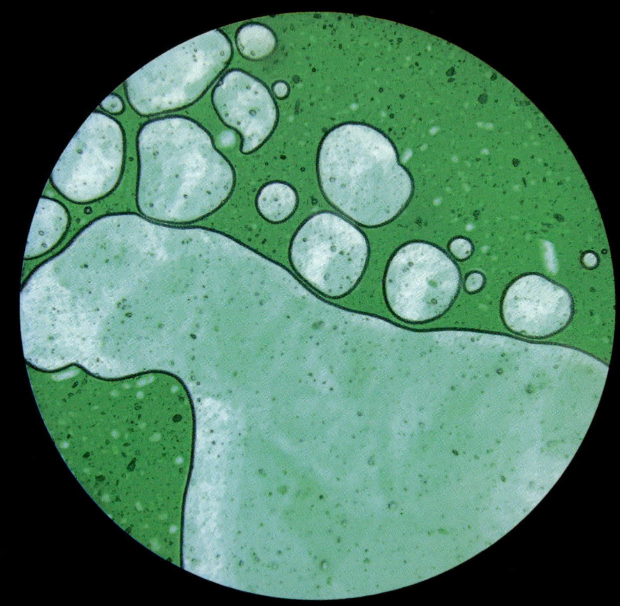

PG7
PHTHALO-
CYANINE
GREEN

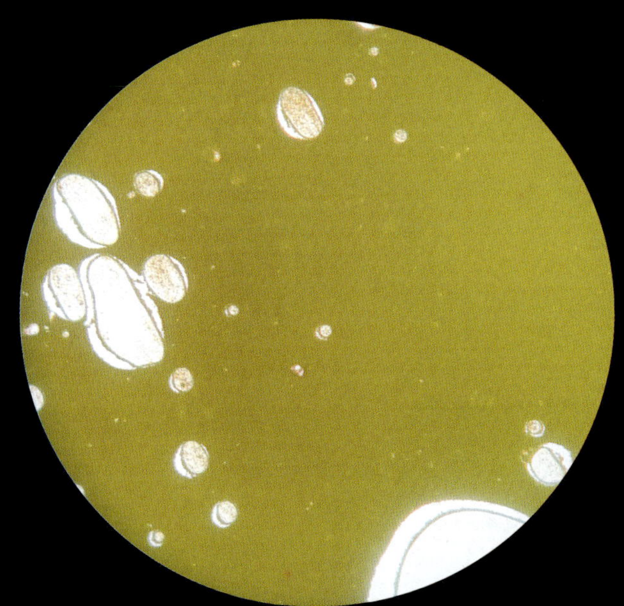

PY42
SYNTHETIC
YELLOW
OCHRE

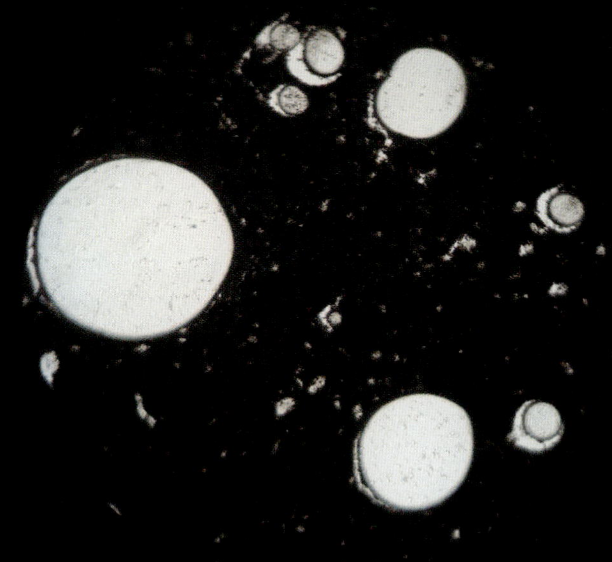

PBK11
MARS BLACK

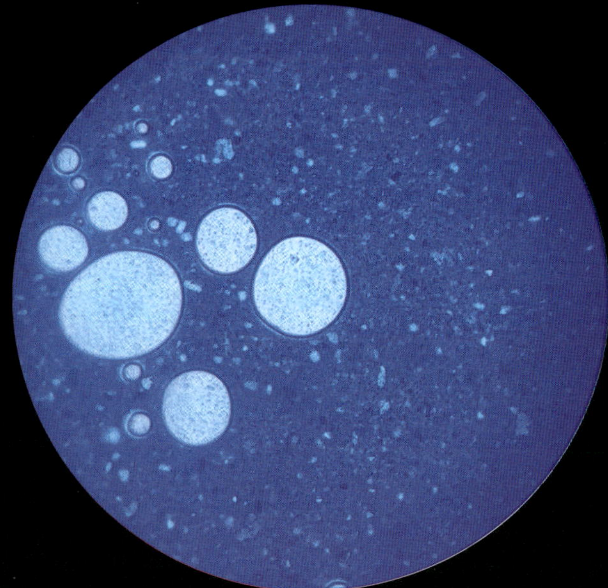

PB29
ULTRAMARINE
BLUE

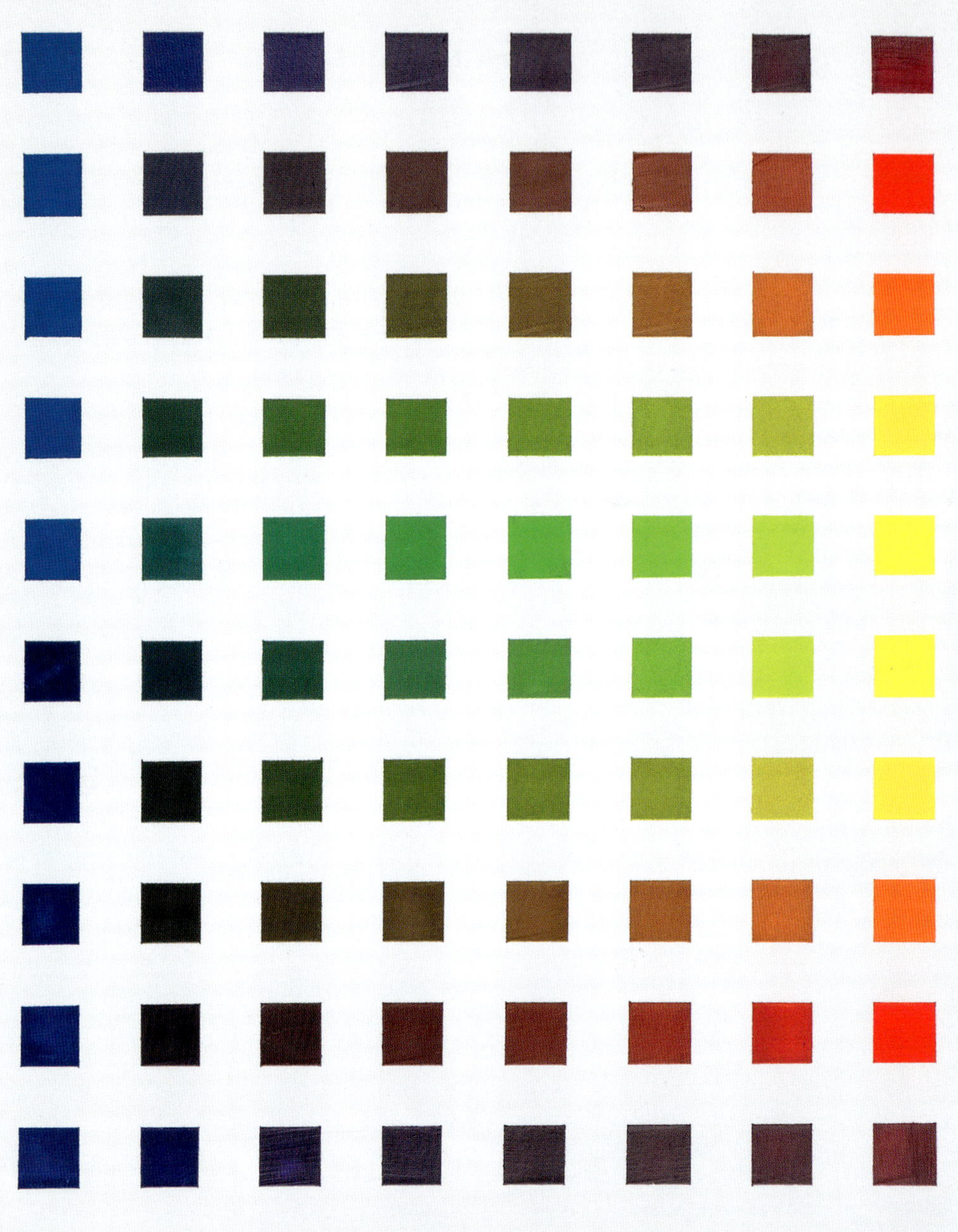

Pigment Library

Here follows a list of the colours I have used in this book. It is by no means an exhaustive list of available colours, and I'm sure many of you might notice some of your personal favourites missing, but it's a good list and hopefully you might discover some new colours among it.

On a good tube of paint, you will find a variety of information. This might include the name of the colour, its lightfastness, opacity/transparency, the oil or binder used, the quantity of paint in millilitres or fluid ounces and the Colour Index Generic Name (from the international database Colour Index) for the pigment used to give the colour in the tube.

Many of these pigments have multiple common names, which is why I've used the Colour Index Generic Name for each of the pigments listed rather than a name.

Each pigment on the Colour Index list has two types of classifications, but as you only regularly find the Colour Index Generic Name code on your tubes of paint, this is the one that is listed below. The code has two parts: letters and then numbers. The letters are P for pigment and a letter for the colour and then there is a number for the specific pigment colour. For example, PB29 is pigment blue 29, which is ultramarine blue.

PY	=	pigment yellow
PO	=	pigment orange
PR	=	pigment red
PV	=	pigment violet
PB	=	pigment blue
PG	=	pigment green
PBr	=	pigment brown
PBk	=	pigment black
PW	=	pigment white

These codes are much more reliable on paint labels than the colour name, as names can vary enormously but pigments and their codes do not. To take a common pigment as an example, PY3 (pigment yellow 3) can be known as antique lemon, arylamide yellow, arylide yellow, blockx yellow, bright yellow lake, brilliant yellow, cadmium lemon azo, cadmium lemon hue, hansa yellow, helios yellow, Japanese yellow lemon, lemon yellow, permanent lemon, primary yellow, primrose yellow, Scheveningen yellow lemon, studio yellow, titanium yellow (hue), Turner's yellow (hue), Winsor lemon and zinc yellow hue.

The Colour Index Online (colour-index.com) is published by the Society of Dyers and Colourists (SDC) and American Association of Textile Chemists and Colorists (AATCC).

If a colour has a significant visual difference when painted thin or when white is added, I've added an extra square to demonstrate this. If there is only one square like for PY3 or PO73, this is because it is much the same hue whether seen thick or thin, and adding white doesn't do anything particularly exciting either. It will usually be the darker transparent colours that get three squares.

Transparent colours, such as PR122, PB15, PG7, PB29 and PV23, are very dark when squeezed from the tube but can be seen at their peak saturation and vibrancy when brushed very thinly, used as a wash or glaze over a white surface, or have white added to them. Otherwise, due to their excellent tinting ability, they are predominantly used in mixes.

As a rule, all primary and secondary colours are slow to dry and all oxides (earths) are fast to dry, but as with every rule, there are exceptions.

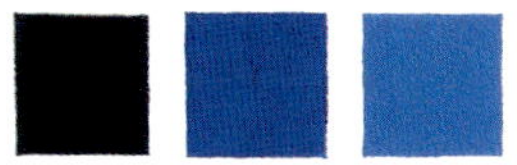

PB15:1 Phthalocyanine blue. Transparent. Cool. Sold as a range of hues from PB15:1 to PB15:6. PB15:1 is the commonest. An excellent, economical colour used industrially as well as for artists' paint. Useful for cool blue mixes. Slow drying.

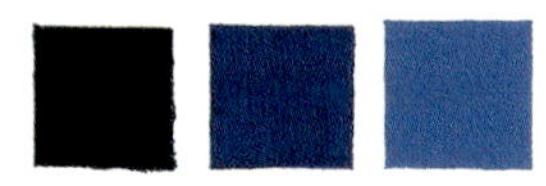

PR27 Prussian blue. Transparent. Greenish blue. Unique colour with a metallic aroma. Fast drying.

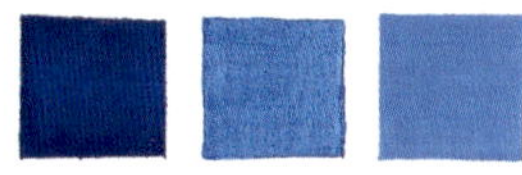

PB28 Cobalt blue. Warm to almost neutral visually. Transparent to semi-transparent. A good mid-value blue, but usually expensive. Mixes well. Fast drying. PB15 is a cheaper substitute for PB28 if mixed with PB29 and perhaps white.

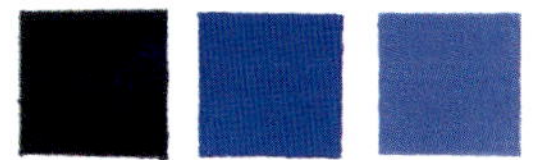

PB29 Ultramarine blue. Transparent. Usually warm. From the Latin for 'over the sea', as it was originally extracted from lapis lazuli minerals from Afghanistan. The modern (mid-19th-century) synthetic equivalent is much cheaper than the original, and an excellent colour, widely used in industry as well as in artists' paint. Great mixer. The warm equivalent to PB15 in many ways. My favourite blue. Slow drying.

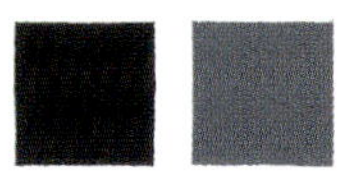

PBk11 Mars black. Opaque. Fast to medium drying, as it's an iron oxide. Possibly the most neutral black. Odd fact: it can be attracted to a magnet. My personal favourite.

PBk9 Ivory black.
Opaque to semi-opaque.
Cool to neutral and more
subtle than some blacks.
Used to be made from
burnt ivory, now made
from burnt animal bones,
so non-vegan. Slow drying.

PBk6 Lamp black.
Opaque. Cool.
Made from soot.
Very slow drying.

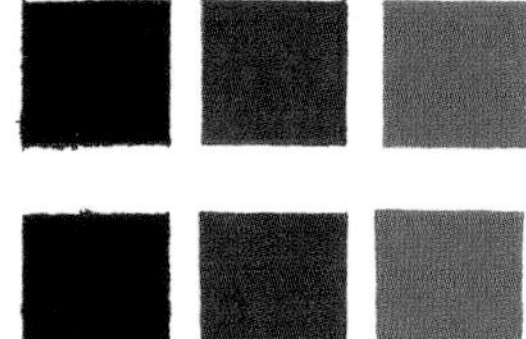

**PBr7 Burnt umber, raw
umber, brown ochre,
etc.** Semi-transparent,
but with excellent
covering ability and
fast drying. This iron-
oxide pigment comes
in a range of hues from
warm reddish-brown
to greenish-brown. The
difference between the
warm orange/red burnt
umber and the generally
greenish raw umber is
that the pigment in burnt
umber has actually been
burnt (calcined), turning
it redder in nature.
Raw umber contains
manganese. Like most
iron oxides, it dries fast.

PBr8 Van Dyke brown.
If genuine, a great choice
for neutral grey mixes,
but gritty in nature
compared to a synthetic
iron oxide and not widely
available, perhaps due to
problematic performance.
Slow drying.

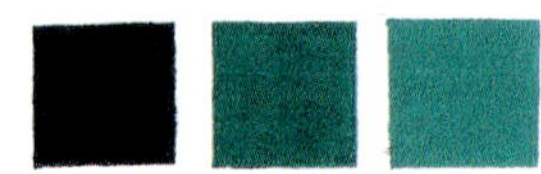

P(03) Payne's grey.
Possibly the colour with
the widest variety of
hues, values and recipes
of any colour on the
market. There doesn't
seem to be a fixed
recipe for Payne's grey.
There are at least eleven
different manufactured
versions on the market.
Recipes include any of
the following: PBk11,
PB60, PBk9, PB29, PY42,
PBk7, PV19, PB15, PW6,
PBk6. I've included
this colour more as an
example of vague colour
recipes for paint names
than a usable paint. It
might save time if you
like a particular brand
to have a tube, but
otherwise mix your own.

**PG7 Phthalocyanine
green.** Transparent.
Cool. A unique, powerful,
bluish-green. Great
mixer, very dark *en masse*,
but vibrant green as a
glaze or tint. A much
more vibrant substitute
for genuine viridian
green (PG18), which
I found disappointing.

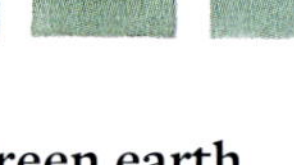

**PG23 Green earth
(terre verte).**
Transparent. Cool.
Very weak colour. Not
a fan – perhaps too
subtle for me. Medium
to slow drying.

**PG50 Cobalt titanate
blue/green.** Also known
as cobalt teal and
turquise. Opaque. Cool.
A unique and beautiful
colour with excellent
covering ability. The
opacity is similar to
phthalocyanine blue +
green (PG7) mixed with
titanium white. One of
those 'is it blue or is it
green?' hues. An almost
identical equivalent
can be mixed with the
previously mentioned
colours. Slow drying.

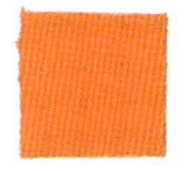

PO73 Pyrrole orange. Semi-transparent. An excellent single-pigment orange with good mixing abilities. Slow drying.

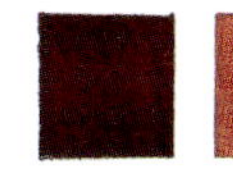 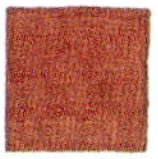 

PR83 Alizarin crimson. Transparent. Cool. Wonderful name, less-wonderful pigment. Derived from the madder genus of plants. One of the few organic pigments still widely in use. It is fugitive in nature, so prone to fade in glazes and washes or to darken in sunlight. There are many permanent versions of this colour available. I'd advise choosing one of those. Slow drying.

 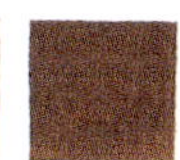 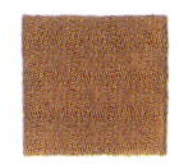

PR101 Synthetic iron oxide red. Also sold as, or used in, transparent oxide red, Venetian red and burnt sienna, among others. An excellent, mostly opaque to semi-opaque and fast-drying pigment. Comes in a range of warm orange-brown to cool purplish-brown hues. Fast drying.

PR108 Cadmium red. Opaque. Warm. Like cadmium yellow (PY35), can come in a range of hues from very warm to darker and cooler. Usually expensive, but worth the investment. Excellent covering ability. Very slow drying.

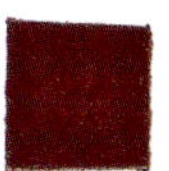 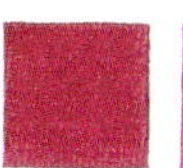 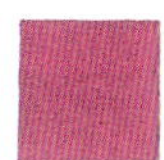

PR122 Quinacridone magenta. Transparent. Cool. One of the best cool reds and a good base for many colours requiring a cool red. Makes vivid pinks if mixed carefully with titanium white (PW6). Usually inexpensive. Slow drying.

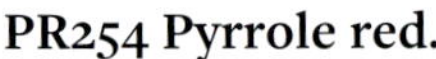

PR254 Pyrrole red.
Opaque (can be semi-transparent depending on manufacturer). Warm to neutral. Usually an excellent substitute for cadmium red. Slow drying.

PY3 Arylide or hansa yellow. Transparent to semi-transparent. Cool. Good mixer in primary and secondary colours due to its relative transparency. Slow drying.

PY35 Cadmium yellow. Opaque. Can come in many hues of yellow from cool lemon yellow to a warm, almost orange yellow. Excellent covering ability, but like all cadmiums, expensive and very slow to dry.

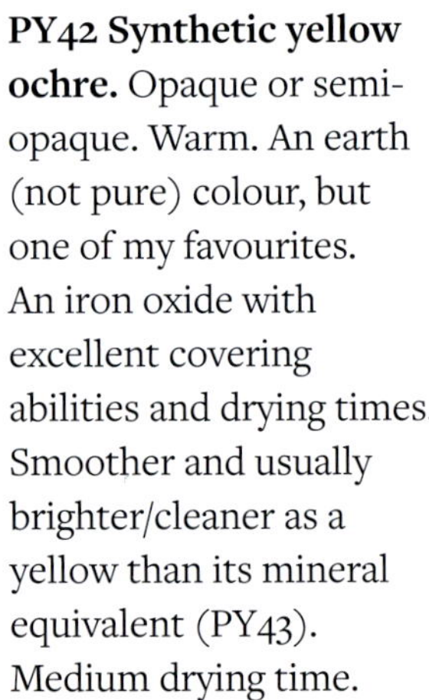

PY42 Synthetic yellow ochre. Opaque or semi-opaque. Warm. An earth (not pure) colour, but one of my favourites. An iron oxide with excellent covering abilities and drying times. Smoother and usually brighter/cleaner as a yellow than its mineral equivalent (PY43). Medium drying time.

PY43 Natural yellow ochre. Opaque or semi-opaque. Warm. Extracted from pulverised rock (limonite), so slightly gritty compared to PY42. Sometimes mixed with PY42, as they are almost identical chemically. Some brands can be very gritty, some less so. Not ideal on a glass palette. Medium drying time.

PY43/42 Raw sienna (can be either PY42, PY43, both or mixed with PR101, or purely PBr7). Opaque or semi-opaque. Warm. Practically the same colour as yellow ochre, but usually slightly darker. A colour I would mix rather than buy.

Pigments *and* Paints

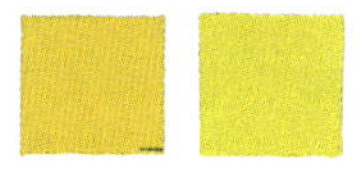

PY73/74 Arylide or hansa yellow.
Transparent. Usually warm. Often sold as a warm cadmium hue/substitute. Good mixer like PY3. Slow drying.

PW1 Lead white. Opaque. Warm. Fast drying. Restricted availability due to its toxicity, but a very interesting white to use.

PW4 Zinc white. Semi-opaque. Cool. Good mixer for a white, as it doesn't dull colours as much as titanium white, but possibly problematic in terms of longevity, as it might degrade in certain circumstances. Often added to titanium white. Slow drying.

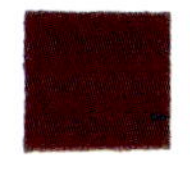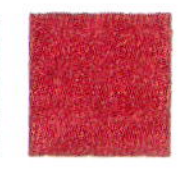

PW6 Titanium white. Opaque. Cool. The most used white. Excellent all-rounder as a white. May be a carcinogen if inhaled as dust. Slow drying.

PV19 Quinacridone violet (permanent rose). Transparent. Warm. A warmer, redder version of PR122 and so a link in terms of hue between magenta (PR122) and warmer reds such as PR254 and PR108. Makes very vibrant pinks when mixed with white.

PV23 Dioxazine violet. Transparent. Warm/cool. One of the darkest colours available that isn't a black. Makes vibrant purple/violet tints when mixed with white. Slow to medium drying.

Index

colour adjacency 113–14
colour adjacency and
bias 100–4
green earth (terre verte)
(PG23) 153, 164
hue 30–4
phthalocyanine green
(PG7) 48, 61, 66, 76, 84,
156, 164
RGB (red, green and
blue) 88–9
RYB (red, yellow and
blue) 93, 96
saturation 66, 67
temperature 68–72, 74
transparency and opacity
76, 84
using colour biases when
mixing colours 106–11
greys 22, 37, 46, 49, 52, 53,
58, 62, 74, 163
altering a colour's value
40
CMY (cyan, magenta and
yellow) 91
greyscale 19
grisaille 57
mixing colours 110–11
Payne's grey (P(o3)) 164
saturation 54–5, 64–5
volume and weight 124,
129
greyscale 19

grisaille 57
ground 19

H
hansa or arylide yellow
(PY73/74) 84, 160,
166,167
Helmholtz, Hermann von 88
Hering, Ewald 21
HSL 27
HSV 27
hue 19, 30–4
hydrous aluminium
potassium silicate 149

I
impossible colours 19
indigo 33
interactions of colour 119
transitions and form
132–43
volume and weight
120–30
International Commission
on Illumination 30
Itten, Johannes *The Elements
of Color* 68
ivory black (PBk9) 150, 153,
163

K
kaolin 149

L
lamp black (PBk6) 153, 163
lead white (PW1) 40, 77,
153, 167
Linnaean classification 34

M
magenta 47, 61, 76, 78, 84,
95–6, 109, 113, 129–30
CMY (cyan, magenta and
yellow) 91
quinacridone magenta
(PR122) 79, 91, 165
marble dust 149
Mars black (PBk11) 57, 62,
64, 157, 162
mass tone 19
Maxwell, James Clark 22, 88
medium 19
mica 149
mixing colours 100–4
colour adjacency 113–15
colour biases 106–11
Munsell, A.H. 18, 27, 52,
62, 65

N
Natural Colour System
(NCS) 27
natural yellow ochre (PY43)
154–5, 166
neutral 19
Newton, Isaac *Opticks* 22, 33

Acknowledgements

If I have had any insight or inspiration regarding patterns in colour that have been there since the inception of the universe, then rather than take credit for being very clever personally, I would give thanks to God for helping me to gain insight into what was already there. The flaws and mistakes I'm happy to take the credit for.

As for the rest, I really do stand on the shoulders of giants who have gone before me, and I build on their work: Isaac Newton, Johann Wolfgang von Goethe, Johannes Itten, Philipp Otto Runge, James Clerk Maxwell, Hermann von Helmholtz and Olafur Eliasson.

In true Oscars style, I would also like to acknowledge and honour some family and friends, with whose love and support I've been able to make this book a reality:

Michelle, my wife, without whose encouragement and patient endurance while listening to endless hours of colour information (especially late at night, when she wanted to go to sleep) this book would never have been made.

My wonderful family has always encouraged and supported me in my artistic efforts. There aren't the words to express my love and thanks to you all. Special mention needs to be made of my son Josiah (Joe), whose help and advice helped shape some key design decisions on the book.

Ellie Corbett, for her incredible skills in taking all the disjointed information and diagrams I sent her and turning them into a book that actually made sense, and Ben Gardiner, Ben Hawkins, Rachel Silverlight and Caroline Alberti for their amazing editorial, design and production work.

My great friend Hans van der Leeuw, for his friendship and encouragement over the years.

Jake Spicer, for the publishing masterclass, help and encouragement, and for being brave and kind enough to tell me when I was wrong.

Peter James Field, Grey Simpson and Paul Bhajjan, for reading and advising on my early attempts to write a book.

François Schaal, for being generous and giving me so much valuable information from behind the curtain of the paint-making industry.

Professor Matthias Keller from the Department of Physics at the University of Sussex, for his patient help and assistance. Michael Harding, for great book suggestions and David Coles of Langridge. Liesel and Ronan at Cass Art, and Stephanie and the lab at Winsor & Newton.

Sharon Campbell for her patience and almost magical photography skills.

My amazing Instagram followers and friends who patiently let me share my ideas and discoveries, and who, through their questions and comments (even the critical ones), have helped shape my understanding of colour and therefore this book.

Also:
Chris Osborne
Nasim Lashgari
Lauren Morse
Felicity Price-Smith
Alex Willis
Melissa Carmon and Jonathan Myers of www.thepaintlist.com
www.artiscreation.com

And (insert name here), who is no doubt thinking, 'Where's my mention?' – who I have totally forgotten and will kick myself later for not including.

Finally to you, dear reader, if you've got this far and read the book. Thank you.

First published in Great Britain in 2024
by Ilex, an imprint of
Octopus Publishing Group Ltd
Carmelite House
50 Victoria Embankment
London EC4Y 0DZ
www.octopusbooks.co.uk

An Hachette UK Company
www.hachette.co.uk

The authorized representative in
the EEA is Hachette Ireland
8 Castlecourt Centre, Dublin 15
D15 XTP3, Ireland (email: info@hbgi.ie)

Text and artworks copyright
© Ian Goldsmith 2024
Design and layout copyright
© Octopus Publishing Group 2024

ISBN 978-1-78157-902-2

A CIP catalogue record for this book is
available from the British Library.

Printed and bound in China

10 9 8 7 6 5 4 3

Consultant Editorial Director:
Ellie Corbett
Managing Editor: Rachel Silverlight
Project Editor: Ben Hawkins
Editorial Assistant: Ellen Sleath
Art Director: Ben Gardiner
Designer: Geoff Fennell
Production Manager: Caroline Alberti